anythink

D0688913

Apréndete tus números/Know Your Numbers

Una bandera a cuadros
Un libro para contar sobre carreras de autos

One Checkered Flag
A Counting Book About Racing

por/by **Michael Dahl**

ilustrado por/illustrated by **Derrick Alderman & Denise Shea**

traducción/translation: **Dr. Martín Luis Guzmán Ferrer**

PICTURE WINDOW BOOKS
a capstone imprint

Special thanks to our advisers for their expertise:
Stuart Farm, M.Ed.
Mathematics Lecturer
University of North Dakota, Grand Forks

Susan Kesselring, M.A.
Literacy Educator
Rosemount–Apple Valley–Eagan (Minnesota) School District

The editor would like to thank Nichole Fredrickson Nelson of Elko Speedway for her expert advice in preparing this book.

Editor: Brenda Haugen
Spanish Copy Editor: Adalín Torres-Zayas
Designer: Nathan Gassman
Book Designer: Eric Manske
Production Specialist: Jane Klenk
The illustrations in this book were created digitally.

Picture Window Books
151 Good Counsel Drive
P.O. Box 669
Mankato, MN 56002-0669
877-845-8392
www.capstonepub.com

 All books published by Picture Window Books are manufactured with paper containing at least 10 percent post-consumer waste.

Library of Congress Cataloging-in-Publication Data
Dahl, Michael.
    Una bandera a cuadros : un libro para contar sobre carreras de autos / por Michael Dahl = One checkered flag : a counting book about racing / by Michael Dahl.
        p. cm.—(Apréndete tus números = Know your numbers)
    Summary: "A counting book featuring things found at a car race, from one black-and-white checkered flag to twelve reporters. Readers are invited to find hidden numbers on an illustrated activity page—in both English and Spanish"—Provided by publisher.
    ISBN 978-1-4048-6295-1 (library binding)
    1. Counting—Juvenile literature. 2. Automobile racing—Juvenile literature. I. Title. II. Title: One checkered flag.
QA113 .D3547 2011
513.2'11—dc22   2010009873

Printed in the United States of America in North Mankato, Minnesota.
012011 006047R

TWELVE reporters wait for the race to start.

DOCE reporteros esperan el inicio de la carrera.

3

ELEVEN autographs
decorate the program.

11

4

ONCE autógrafos
adornan el programa.

TEN spoilers glitter and gleam.

DIEZ despojadores destellan y brillan.

NINE safety helmets are strapped on tight.

NUEVE cascos de seguridad están sujetos muy ajustados.

EIGHT binoculars follow the race.

OCHO binoculares siguen la carrera.

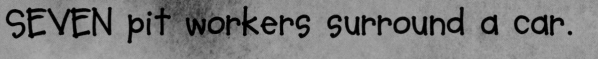

SEVEN pit workers surround a car.

SIETE ayudantes rodean al auto en el foso.

SIX empty gas cans sit in a row.

6

12

SEIS latas vacías de gasolina están en línea.

FIVE racecars lead the pack.

CINCO autos de carreras
van al frente de la jauría.

15

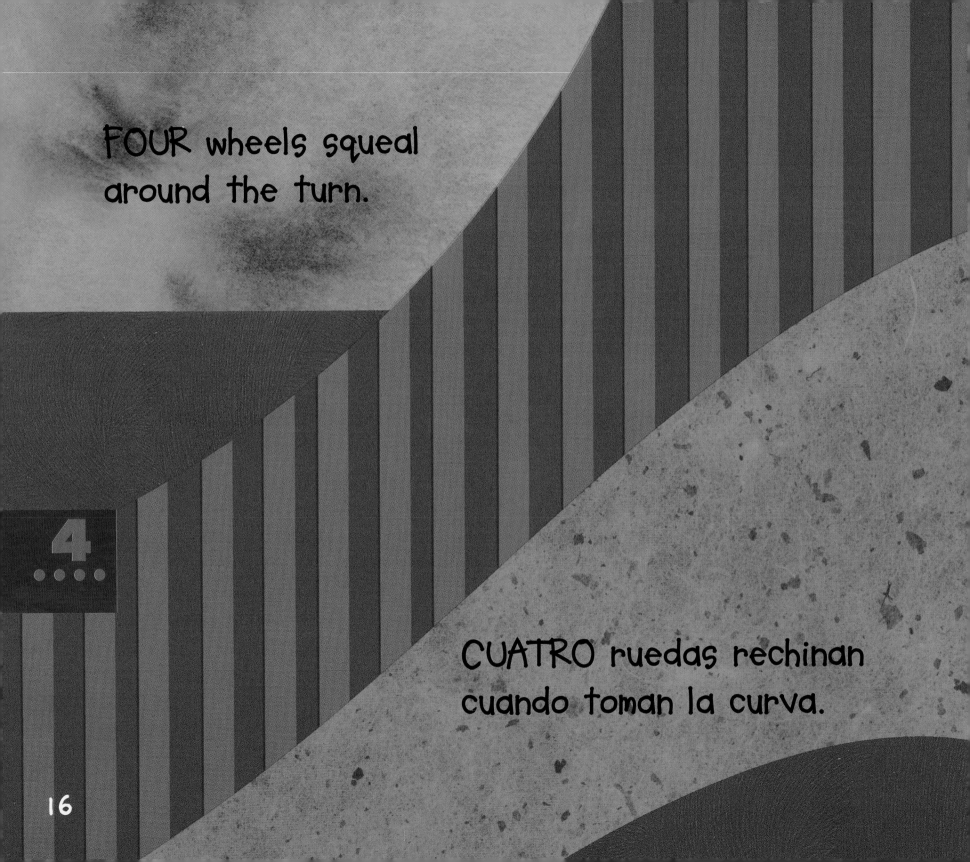

FOUR wheels squeal around the turn.

4

CUATRO ruedas rechinan cuando toman la curva.

THREE grandstands hold the fans.

TRES gradas contienen a los aficionados.

TWO drivers race for the finish line.

DOS conductores corren hacia la meta.

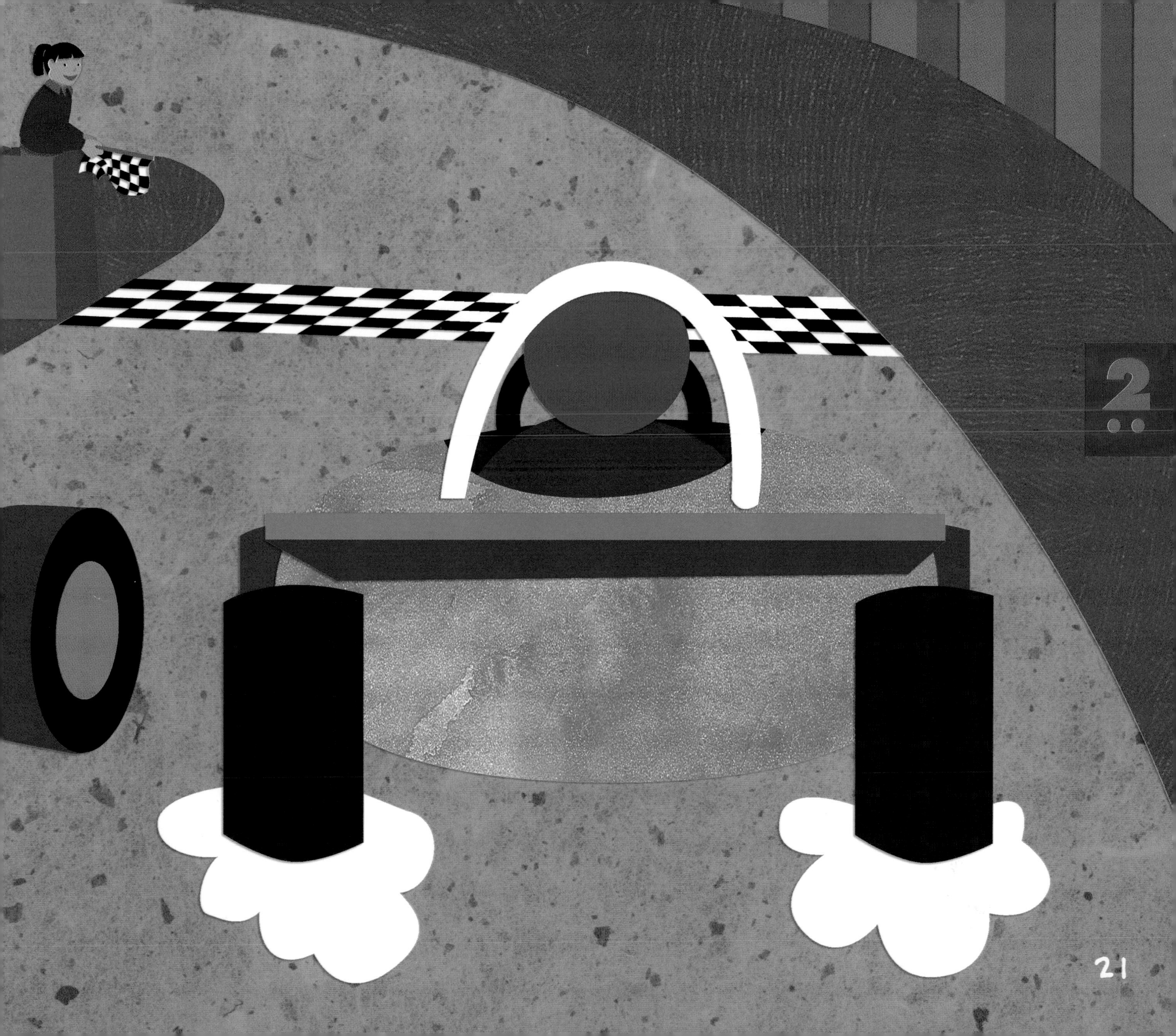
2

ONE black-and-white checkered flag waves wildly.

THE WINNER!

UNA bandera a cuadros negra y blanca ondea desenfrenadamente.

¡EL GANADOR!

Fun Facts

 The spoiler is on the back of the car. The spoiler pushes air down and helps the car's tires stay on the racetrack.

 Drivers wear helmets and special clothing that doesn't catch fire easily. Lap and shoulder belts also help keep drivers safe.

 Race cars hold fuel in special tanks. The tanks contain foam or spongy materials to keep the fuel from spraying around if the cars crash.

Find the Numbers

Now you have finished reading the story, but a surprise still awaits you. Hidden in each picture is one of the numbers from 1 to 12. Can you find them all?

12 – on the purple car
11 – on the metal band of the pencil
10 – on the steering wheel of the second car from the left
9 – on the yellow helmet
8 – on the shirt on the man that is top left
7 – on the leg of the woman on page 10
6 – near the back of the car
5 – back wheel of leading car
4 – left front tire
3 – front left corner of right grandstand section
2 – back left tire on orange car
1 – bottom right corner of flag person's stand

Internet Sites

FactHound offers a safe, fun way to find Internet sites related to this book. All of the sites on FactHound have been researched by our staff.
Here's all you do:
Visit *www.facthound.com*
Type in this code: 9781404862951

Datos divertidos

 El despojador está en la parte trasera del coche. El despojador empuja el aire hacia abajo y sirve para que las llantas se queden en la pista.

 Los conductores usan cascos y ropa especial para repeler el fuego. Los cinturones del asiento y la puerta también son para la seguridad del conductor.

 Los autos de carreras tienen tanques especiales para la gasolina. Los tanques contienen espuma o materiales absorbentes que impiden que el combustible se extienda en caso de un choque.

Encuentra los números

Ahora que ya terminaste de leer el cuento, aún te espera una sorpresa. En cada ilustración se encuentra escondido un número del 1 al 12. ¿Puedes encontrarlos a todos?

12 – en el coche morado
11 – en la bandita de metal del lápiz
10 – en el volante del segundo auto a la izquierda
9 – en el casco amarillo
8 – en la camisa azul del hombre que está arriba a la izquierda
7 – en la pierna de la mujer en la página 10
6 – cerca de la parte trasera del auto
5 – en la rueda trasera del auto que va ganando
4 – en la llanta delantera izquierda
3 – en la esquina inferior en el frente de la sección derecha de las gradas
2 – en la llanta trasera izquierda del auto anaranjado
1 – en la esquina inferior derecha de la persona en las gradas con la bandera

Sitios de Internet

FactHound brinda una forma segura y divertida de encontrar sitios de Internet relacionados con este libro. Todos los sitios en FactHound han sido investigados por nuestro personal.
Esto es todo lo que tienes que hacer:
Visita *www.facthound.com*
Ingresa este código: 9781404862951

IGNE NATURA RENOVATUR INTEGRA

DIDIER CONVARD

DENIS FALQUE - PIERRE WACHS

Couleurs : PAUL

Couverture : ANDRÉ JUILLARD

I.N.R.I
LE TRIANGLE SECRET

TOME IV
Résurrection

Le Triangle Secret :

T. 1 : LE TESTAMENT DU FOU

T. 2 : LE JEUNE HOMME AU SUAIRE

T. 3 : DE CENDRE & D'OR

T. 4 : L'EVANGILE OUBLIÉ

T. 5 : L'INFÂME MENSONGE

T. 6 : LA PAROLE PERDUE

T. 7 : L'IMPOSTEUR

I.N.R.I.

T. 1 : LE SUAIRE

T. 2 : LA LISTE ROUGE

T. 3 : LE TOMBEAU D'ORIENT

T. 4 : RÉSURRECTION

HERTZ

www.glenat.com

© 2007, Éditions Glénat - BP 177 - 38008 GRENOBLE CEDEX
Tous droits réservés pour tous pays
Dépôt légal avril 2007.
ISBN: 978-2-7234-5463-6
Achevé d'imprimer en Belgique en mars 2007 par Lesaffre.

JE REVIENS AVEC HUGUES ET LE CONDUIS IMMÉDIATEMENT À CET APPARTEMENT.

TU REMETS CE PLI EN MAIN PROPRE AU COMTE, PUIS TU FAIS COMME CONVENU.

C'EST CELA, PARS MAINTENANT POUR NE PAS ÊTRE VU ET RASSURE LES AUTRES. QU'ILS M'ATTENDENT AVEC LES CHEVAUX SOUS LA FENÊTRE. NOUS AURONS TRÈS PEU DE TEMPS POUR AGIR... AH, UN DÉTAIL !

OUI, LEQUEL ?

TU AS DU SANG SUR TA MANCHE GAUCHE, NETTOIE-LA AVANT DE TE PRÉSENTER AU COMTE.

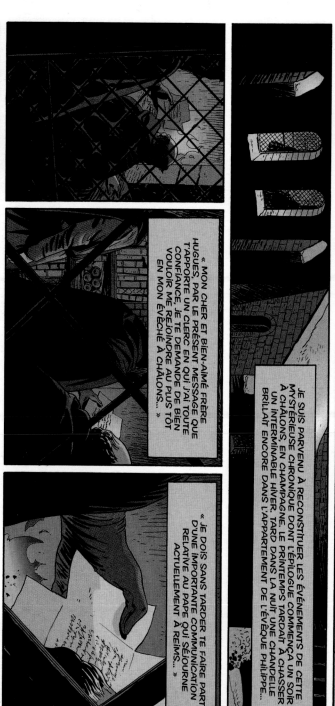

« MON CHER ET BIEN-AIMÉ FRÈRE HUGUES, PAR LE PRÉSENT MESSAGE QUE T'APPORTE UN CLERC EN QUI J'AI TOUTE CONFIANCE, JE TE DEMANDE DE BIEN VOULOIR ME REJOINDRE AU PLUS TÔT EN MON ÉVÊCHÉ À CHÂLONS... »

« JE DOIS SANS TARDER TE FAIRE PART D'UNE IMPORTANTE COMMUNICATION RELATIVE AU PAPE QUI SÉJOURNE ACTUELLEMENT À REIMS... »

JE SUIS PARVENU À RECONSTITUER LES ÉVÉNEMENTS DE CETTE MYSTÉRIEUSE CHRONIQUE DONT L'ÉPILOGUE COMMENÇA UN SOIR À CHÂLONS, EN CHAMPAGNE. LE PRINTEMPS TARDAIT À CHASSER UN INTERMINABLE HIVER. TARD DANS LA NUIT, UNE CHANDELLE BRILLAIT ENCORE DANS L'APPARTEMENT DE L'ÉVÊQUE PHILIPPE...

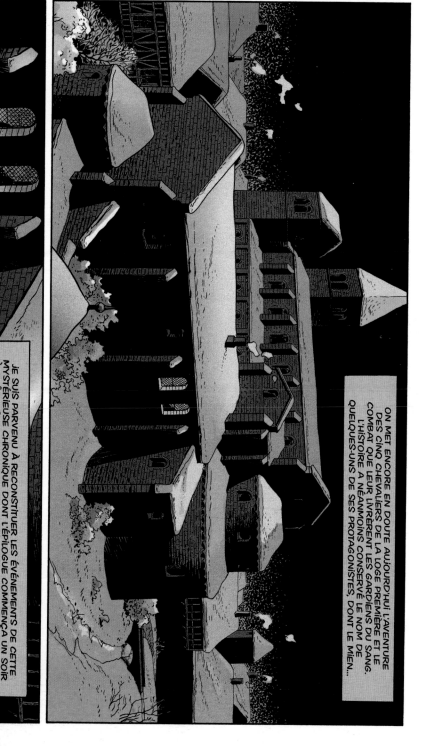

ON MET ENCORE EN DOUTE AUJOURD'HUI L'AVENTURE DES CINQ CHEVALIERS DE LA LOGE PREMIÈRE ET LE COMBAT QUE LEUR LIVRÈRENT LES GARDIENS DU SANG. L'HISTOIRE A NÉANMOINS CONSERVÉ LE NOM DE QUELQUES-UNS DE SES PROTAGONISTES, DONT LE MIEN...

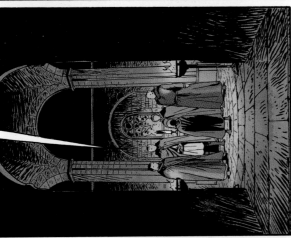

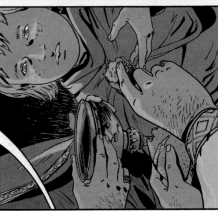

TU VEUX ME FAIRE MOURIR DE FROID, PAPA !

NOUS AVONS UNE RUDE JOURNÉE À REMPLIR, FILS. SORS DE TES DRAPS, RESPIRE UNE LONGUE GOULÉE DE CE BEL AIR FRAIS ET LAVE-TOI DU MUSEAU AU CUL !

NE CROIS PAS CELA... UN CAVALIER VIENT DE PASSER LA POTERNE.

JE COMMENCE À REGRETTER MA CONDITION D'ENFANT... JE TROUVE LE CHANGEMENT DE STATUT UN PEU BRUTAL ! TOUTE LA MAISONNÉE DORT ENCORE À POINGS FERMÉS.

MON CHER ET BIEN-AIMÉ FRÈRE HUGUES, PAR LE PRÉSENT MESSAGE QUE T'APPORTE UN CLERC EN QUI J'AI TOUTE CONFIANCE, JE TE DEMANDE DE BIEN VOULOIR ME REJOINDRE AU PLUS TÔT EN MON ÉVÊCHÉ À CHÂLONS...

LE LENDEMAIN...

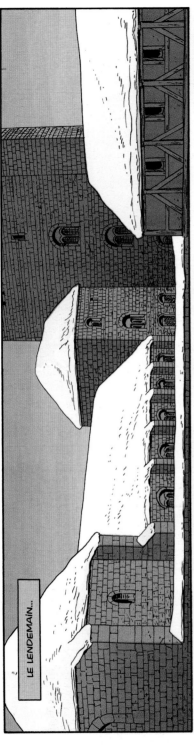

HÉ !

L'HEURE DU COQ ! LA MEILLEURE POUR SE LEVER.

DOIS-JE FAIRE TOUT CELA DE SI BON MATIN ?

MAINTENANT QUE TU ES FRÈRE DE LA LOGE PREMIÈRE, TU DOIS EN ADOPTER AUSSI LA DISCIPLINE. CHAQUE HEURE DU JOUR EST UNE BÉNÉDICTION DE LA VIE. J'AI PRÉVU DE T'EMMENER VISITER LE CHANTIER EN FORÊT D'ORIENT. MAÎTRE ÉLIPHAS A PRESQUE ACHEVÉ LE TOMBEAU.

QUE SE PASSE-T-IL, CHÉRI ?

PHILIPPE M'ÉCRIT, CONSTANCE. CELA DOIT ÊTRE IMPORTANT POUR QU'IL DÉPÊCHE UN PORTEUR SI TÔT.

COMTE HUGUES ? JE SUIS PORTEUR D'UN MESSAGE URGENT DE VOTRE FRÈRE, ÉVÊQUE DE CHÂLONS.

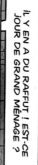

J'AI TROUVÉ CETTE RUSE POUR VOUS FAIRE VENIR À MOI, COMTE. J'ÉTAIS CERTAIN QUE VOUS MORDRIEZ À L'HAMEÇON.

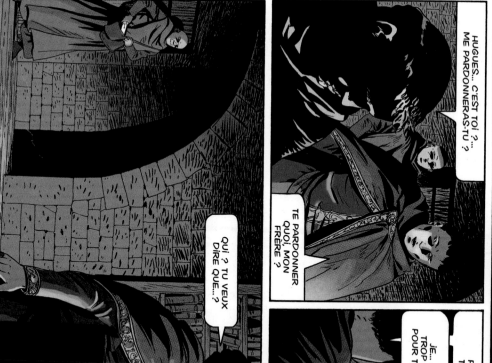

QUI ? TU VEUX DIRE QUE...?

HUGUES... C'EST TOI ?... ME PARDONNERAS-TU ?

TE PARDONNER QUOI, MON FRÈRE ?

JE... J'AI ÉCRIT... J'AVAIS TROP MAL... IL M'A DICTÉ... POUR TE TENDRE UN PIÈGE...

PAR SAINT JEAN, TU ES ATTACHÉ !

ET TU AS ÉTÉ BATTU ! MON PAUVRE FRÈRE, QUE T'EST-IL ARRIVÉ ?

FUIS !... IL... IL EST LÀ, FUIS DONC, PHILIPPE...

LE TEMPS NOUS ÉTAIT CLÉMENT ET LE MESSAGE APPORTÉ PAR VOTRE CLERC EXIGEAIT QUE NOUS NOUS HÂTIONS.

AVEZ-VOUS FAIT BONNE ROUTE ? TROYES N'EST GUÈRE À PORTÉE DE MAIN DE CHÂLONS.

NOTRE CLERC ? VOUS PARLEZ DE CET HOMME QUI EST MONTÉ AVEC LE COMTE ?

EN EFFET, JE PARLE BIEN DE LUI. IL EST ARRIVÉ À MATINES AU COMTÉ ET NOUS AVONS SAUTÉ AUSSITÔT SUR NOS SELLES.

AUCUNE RETRAITE POSSIBLE, HUGUES, VOTRE HEURE EST VENUE, JE DOIS PRENDRE LA BAGUE QUE VOUS PORTEZ À LA MAIN DROITE, VOUS VOYEZ, JE MOISSONNE POUR PRÉSERVER LES INTÉRÊTS DE LA SAINTE ÉGLISE !

MES HOMMES SONT EN BAS, ET...

NON !! PAS MON FRÈRE !

... D'ABORD LE TÉMOIN !

HUGUES ! RÉPONDS-MOI, MON AMI ! JE T'EN PRIE, RÉPONDS !

UN GUET-APENS ! AVEC MOI, VOUS TROIS, VITE ! ÉPÉE EN MAIN, LE COMTE EST EN DANGER DE MORT !

QUOI ? CE MESSAGER N'APPARTIENT PAS À LA MAISON DE L'ÉVÊQUE ?

NULLEMENT, SEIGNEUR ! JE PENSAIS QU'IL FAISAIT PARTIE DE VOS GENS...

JE SAIS, ILS N'AURONT PAS LE TEMPS DE VOUS SAUVER. IL ME SUFFIT DE QUELQUES SECONDES POUR FAUCHER...

VOTRE BAGUE, COMTE...

MONSTRE ! IL ÉTAIT INUTILE DE TUER CET INNOCENT !

ALLONS, AUCUNE ÂME N'EST TOTALEMENT VIERGE ! VOTRE FRÈRE CONNAISSAIT LE SECRET ET VOUS L'AVEZ CONDAMNÉ EN LE LUI CONFIANT.

PLACE !

POUR L'AMOUR DU COMTE, NE LAISSEZ PAS S'ENFUIR LE TUEUR !

IN HOC SIGNO VINCE !

CHRIST-ROI ! NOUS ARRIVONS TROP TARD !

LÀ NOTRE MAÎTRE SUR LE SOL... IL BAIGNE DANS SON SANG !

FINISSONS-EN, SES HOMMES MONTENT L'ESCALIER ! ILS VONT FAIRE SAUTER LA PORTE ET...

COMME TU ES EMPRESSÉ, ROBERT ! TU SAIS QUE J'AIME GOÛTER CES INSTANTS... IL FAUT SAVOIR TROUVER DU PLAISIR DANS SON MÉTIER.

SURTOUT QUAND CE MÉTIER EST UN ART SUBTIL...

PFF ! TU N'ES QU'UN VULGAIRE VIANDARD !

NON, COMTE... JE SUIS LE BRAS DE LA VÉRITÉ ! L'ARME DE DIEU !

11

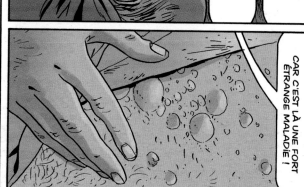

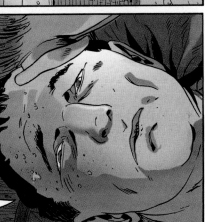
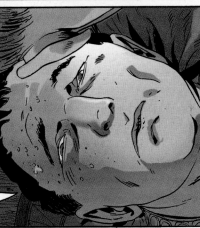

QUE JE SOIS DAMNÉ SI JE N'AI PAS DEVINÉ JUSTE ! LE COMTE HUGUES ET SES CHEVALIERS ONT CERTAINEMENT RAMENÉ CES SYMBOLES DE JÉRUSALEM, ET JE PUIS T'ASSURER QUE CEUX-CI NE SONT PAS AU COMPLET.

JE PASSE POUR UN PIÈTRE DOCTEUR À SES YEUX : LE VIEIL OURS N'EST QUE CLOQUES, ABCÈS ET BUBONS SUR TOUT LE CÔTÉ DROIT. CEPENDANT, SON ESPRIT RESTE VIF ET IL A SU ESQUIVER HABILEMENT LES QUESTIONS QUE JE LUI AI POSÉES AU SUJET DE SES EMPOISONNEURS...

J'AVAIS HÂTE D'ACHEVER CETTE DÉCOCTION À BASE D'ACONITUM CARMICHAELI. MAIS LE PAPE, DIS-MOI, QUELLE MINE AVAIT-IL AUJOURD'HUI ?

TU ES DÉJÀ AU TRAVAIL, MATHIEU ? JE T'AVAIS LAISSÉ ENDORMI COMME UN ANGE ET JE TE RETROUVE LES JOUES EN FEU.

TU NE COMPRENDS PAS ? CES TROIS SIGNES FONT PARTIE D'UNE ÉQUATION ALCHIMIQUE. LA TRADITION HERMÉTIQUE MENTIONNE PARFOIS CELLE-CI COMME ÉTANT LA BASE MÊME DU GRAND MAGISTER !

HMM... COMMENT PEUX-TU L'AFFIRMER ?

LA TRANSMUTATION ?

CE QUE LE PAPE ME DEMANDE DE TRADUIRE EST CERTAINEMENT CELA : LE SECRET DE JÉSUS. L'ANTIQUE MYSTÈRE DE LA RÉSURRECTION...

SACRILÈGE ! JE CROIS AU CHRIST FILS DE DIEU ! JE CROIS QUE C'EST PAR DIEU QUE JÉSUS A TRANSGRESSÉ LA MORT. EX DEO NASCIMUR, IN JESU MORIMUR, PER SPIRITUM SANCTUM REVIVISCIMUS* !

UN SEUL HOMME S'EST RELEVÉ DE LA MORT ET A QUITTÉ SON TOMBEAU... JÉSUS !

ET SI JÉSUS N'AVAIT ÉTÉ QU'UN SIMPLE MORTEL ? S'IL AVAIT ÉTÉ RÉELLEMENT INSTRUIT PAR LES ÉGYPTIENS COMME LE DISENT CERTAINES LÉGENDES ? S'IL AVAIT ÉTÉ LE PREMIER ET LE SEUL À AVOIR CERNÉ LES ARCANES D'UN SAVOIR ANCESTRAL ?

LA TRANSMUTATION DE L'OMBRE EN LUMIÈRE, DU SABLE EN OR, DU MORT EN VIVANT ! LA FORMULE DE L'ELIXIR SPAGIRIQUE !

NON, C'EST IMPOSSIBLE, DENIS ! IMPOSSIBLE...

* DE DIEU NOUS NAISSONS, EN JÉSUS NOUS MOURONS, PAR L'ESPRIT SAINT NOUS REVIVONS !

18

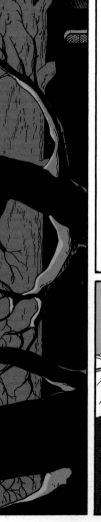

LE COMTE... NOUS AVONS FRAPPÉ DANS LA PROPRE FAMILLE DU ROI ! ET AVEC L'ÉVÊQUE, DANS CELLE DE L'ÉGLISE !

LE ROI NE BOUGERA PAS CAR LES CHAMPENOIS LE TIENDRONT À L'ÉCART DE LEURS AFFAIRES. QUANT À L'ÉGLISE, VOUS EN ÊTES LE MAÎTRE.

TENEZ ! VOICI LE QUATRIÈME DES SAINTS SIGNES. RETIREZ LE MORCEAU DE SUAIRE DE LA CHEVALIÈRE ET, SI VOTRE CONSCIENCE NE VOUS TORTURE PAS TROP, RECOPIEZ-LE COMME VOUS AVEZ FAIT AVEC LES PRÉCÉDENTS.

JE SAIS QUE JE DOIS M'INCLINER SOUS VOS RAILLERIES...

UN DÉMENT ! UN FANATIQUE ! ET JE SUIS CONDAMNÉ À PARTAGER VOTRE FOLIE JUSQU'AU TERME DE VOS CARNAGES !

J'APPELLE CELA UNE ALLIANCE DE RAISON. L'ÉGLISE ET LES GARDIENS DU SANG Y TROUVENT CHACUN LEUR COMPTE, UNE ASSOCIATION SATISFAISANTE JUSQU'À PRÉSENT, NE CROYEZ-VOUS PAS ?

VOS MÉDECINS SONT GENS FORT PRÉVOYANTS, À EN JUGER PAR LA QUANTITÉ DE REMÈDES ET D'ONGUENTS QU'ILS VOUS ONT PRESCRITS POUR UN VULGAIRE RHUMATISME !

NE VOUS SOUCIEZ PAS TANT DE MA SANTÉ. DITES-MOI PLUTÔT SI VOUS AVEZ ENQUÊTÉ SUR LES TRAVAUX QUE DE PAYNS A ENGAGÉS DANS SON DOMAINE, EN FORÊT D'ORIENT.

SOUFFREZ-VOUS, SAINT-PÈRE ? VOTRE MAIN TREMBLE ET VOTRE BRAS SEMBLE GOURD.

CE N'EST RIEN... UN SIMPLE EMBARRAS DÛ AU FROID. LES MURS DE CE PALAIS SUINTENT D'HUMIDITÉ. CE N'EST QUE CELA, RIEN QU'UN RHUMATISME, JE VOUS ASSURE.

J'EXERCE UN CHANTAGE SUR SON CHARPENTIER, MAÎTRE ROGEMOURD. CELUI-CI ME TIENT RÉGULIÈREMENT INFORMÉ DE L'AVANCEMENT DU CHANTIER. IL N'Y A PLUS DE DOUTE, LES CHAMPENOIS CREUSENT UN PROFOND TOMBEAU AU CŒUR DES MARÉCAGES.

LE TOMBEAU DU CHRIST ! ILS EXHUMERONT SA DÉPOUILLE DE L'ENDROIT QU'ILS GARDENT SECRET ET EN TRANSFÉRERONT LES RESTES DANS CE NOUVEAU SÉPULCRE.

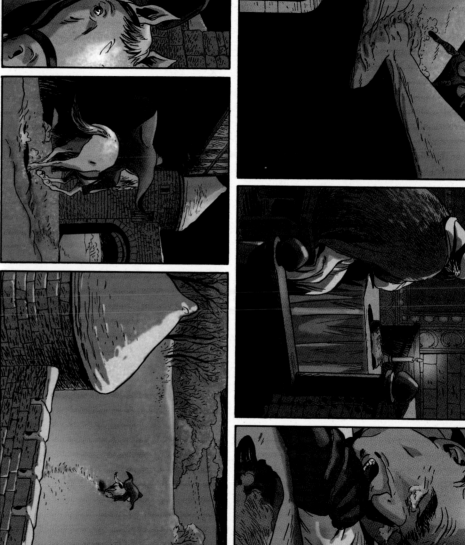

* LORSQU'UN HOMME FORT ET BIEN ARMÉ GARDE SA MAISON, TOUT CE QU'IL POSSÈDE EST EN SÛRETÉ. (ÉVANGILE SELON SAINT LUC, CH. 11)

* SAUVEZ VOTRE PEUPLE, SEIGNEUR, ET BÉNISSEZ VOTRE HÉRITAGE.

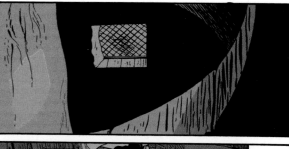

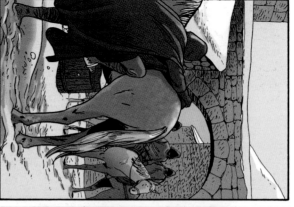

... OUI, UNE BELLE JOURNÉE EN VÉRITÉ ! LOUÉ SOIT DIEU POUR LEQUEL NOUS OFFRONS NOS VIES ET NOS ÂMES, COMPAGNONS !

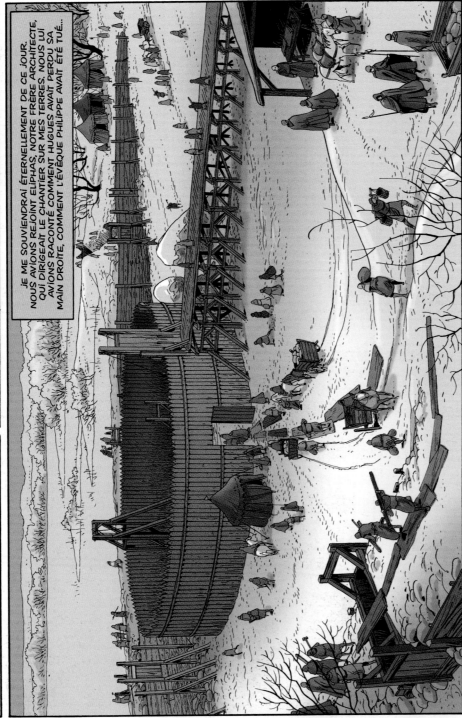

JE ME SOUVIENDRAI ÉTERNELLEMENT DE CE JOUR. NOUS AVIONS REJOINT ELIPHAS, NOTRE FRÈRE ARCHITECTE, QUI DIRIGEAIT LE CHANTIER SUR MES TERRES. NOUS LUI AVIONS RACONTÉ COMMENT HUGUES AVAIT PERDU SA MAIN DROITE, COMMENT L'ÉVÊQUE PHILIPPE AVAIT ÉTÉ TUÉ...

NOUS TERMINONS DE PLACER LES VANNES PAR LESQUELLES NOUS INONDERONS LE TOMBEAU. J'AI PRATIQUÉ DES ESSAIS CONCLUANTS SUR DES MAQUETTES, LE CAVEAU DANS LEQUEL REPOSERA JÉSUS DEMEURERA ÉTANCHE.

TON GÉNIE ME SURPRENDRA TOUJOURS, ELIPHAS, TOUT AUTANT QUE TA MODESTIE !

26

VENEZ, EN ATTENDANT MAÎTRE ROGEMOURD, JE VAIS VOUS MONTRER L'AVANCEMENT DES TRAVAUX. VOYEZ, NOUS AVONS FINI DE CREUSER TOUS LES CANAUX DANS LESQUELS NOUS AVONS RECUEILLI LES EAUX DES MARAIS AVOISINANTS LES PLUS IMPORTANTS.

ET LES DIGUES ONT TOUTES ÉTÉ MONTÉES.

ET LE PAPE, S'EST-IL MANIFESTÉ ?

PAS ENCORE. SANS DOUTE EST-IL TROP ORGUEILLEUX POUR S'ABAISSER À NOUS DEMANDER LE REMÈDE À SON MAL ! OU BIEN N'EST-IL PAS SUFFISAMMENT ATTEINT ? ATTENDONS, IL NOUS APPELLERA.

AU MÊME MOMENT...

PÈRE ! ILS SONT REVENUS... CE SONT EUX !

QUI SONT CES CAVALIERS, MAÎTRE LANDÉRIC ?

NE VOUS EN SOUCIEZ PAS, FINISSEZ LE CHARGEMENT.

SUIS-MOI À L'ÉCART DANS TON ATELIER, LANDÉRIC. J'AI UN SERVICE À TE DEMANDER ET JE SUIS CERTAIN QUE TU NE POURRAS PAS LE REFUSER. TU ES HOMME DE BON SENS À CE QUE JE SAIS.

CELA DÉPEND DU SERVICE, MESSIRE.

ET NIZIER ENCORE BIEN PLUS ! VOIS COMME IL TREMBLE...

TU AS REMARQUÉ ? NOTRE MAÎTRE A SEMBLÉ EFFRAYÉ À LA VUE DE CES INCONNUS.

TU ACCEPTERAS ! CAR TU ES SURTOUT UN PÈRE SOUCIEUX DU BIEN-ÊTRE DE SON FILS. JE VOIS D'AILLEURS QUE NIZIER S'EST REMIS DE SA BLESSURE. IL SERAIT FÂCHEUX QU'IL SOIT DE NOUVEAU AFFLIGÉ.

NON, MESSIRE ! JE NE POURRAI JAMAIS FAIRE CELA AU CHEVALIER DE PAYNS... NON, POUR L'AMOUR DE DIEU ! JE NE PUIS LE TRAHIR.

TON FILS DEMEURERA LÀ AVEC L'UN DE MES HOMMES. IL SERA LE GAGE DE TON OBÉISSANCE. JE TE JURE QUE TU LE RETROUVERAS EN VIE SI TU T'ACQUITTES DE TA TÂCHE SELON MON PLAN.

TU LE FERAS POURTANT, ET TU JOUERAS TON RÔLE AVEC NATUREL AFIN QU'IL NE SE RENDE COMPTE DE RIEN.

VOUS N'AVEZ DONC AUCUNE PITIÉ ?

SI C'ÉTAIT LE CAS, J'AURAIS DÉJÀ TRANCHÉ LA TÊTE DE NIZIER. ALORS, TA RÉPONSE ?

OUI... J'OBÉIRAI... POUR NIZIER MAIS QUE DIEU ME PARDONNE !

29

NIZIER N'EST PAS AVEC VOUS ? IL M'AVAIT POURTANT PROMIS DE VOUS ACCOMPAGNER.

EUH... IL EST DÉSOLÉ, MAURIN... VRAIMENT ! IL SOUFFRE DE LA GORGE À CAUSE D'UN MAUVAIS VENT COULIS QUI TRAVERSE NOTRE ATELIER. J'AI... J'AI PRÉFÉRÉ QU'IL RESTE AU CHAUD.

28

QUANT À MOI, JE VAIS RÉGLER CE QUE NOUS LUI DEVONS. IL A AMPLEMENT MÉRITÉ SON SALAIRE.

VOUS AUTRES, AIDEZ MAÎTRE ROGEMOURD À DÉCHARGER SA CHARRETTE ET PORTEZ AUSSITÔT SES CHARPENTES SUR L'ÎLE.

SEIGNEUR... MON FILS EST GARDÉ EN OTAGE, MON NIZIER ! IL A PROMIS DE LUI LAISSER LA VIE SAUVE SI JE VOUS TRAHISSAIS ET... J'IMPLORE VOTRE CLÉMENCE...

L'HOMME À LA HACHE ! VOUS L'AVEZ FAIT ENTRER DANS LE CHANTIER, ROGEMOURD ! VOUS, LE PRUD'HOMME DE VOTRE GUILDE ? ET VOTRE SERMENT ?!

PEU APRÈS...

QU'IL SE SOIGNE BIEN. APPROCHEZ, MAÎTRE ROGEMOURD, VOTRE ARGENT VOUS ATTEND. VOUS PAIEREZ VOS COMPAGNONS EN LES REMERCIANT POUR LA QUALITÉ DE LEUR OUVRAGE.

JE... JE NE MANQUERAI PAS DE LEUR TRANSMETTRE LE COMPLIMENT, SEIGNEUR DE PAYNS. ILS TOUCHERONT LEUR SOLDE SELON LES JUSTES PRINCIPES DE NOTRE PROFESSION...

AU SECOURS ! PÈRE !

SOYONS PATIENTS, DÈS QUE LES GARDIENS SE SENTIRONT EN SÉCURITÉ, ILS ABANDONNERONT MAURIN, ET NOUS VERRONS CELUI-CI APPARAÎTRE SUR LE CHEMIN. CONFIANCE, MON AMI.

DONNE-MOI LA MAIN, ELIPHAS.

IL NE SE PROTÉGERA PAS TOUJOURS DERRIÈRE UN ENFANT ! SI JAMAIS IL NE TIENT PAS SA PAROLE... S'IL FAIT DU MAL À MAURIN.

IL A DIT QU'IL LE RELÂCHERAIT. IL POSSÈDE MAINTENANT LA DERNIÈRE BAGUE, C'EST TOUT CE QU'IL ÉTAIT VENU CHERCHER.

NON, DE PAYNS ! CE SERAIT TROP DANGEREUX... ET QUE PERSONNE NE BOUGE, IL EN VA DE LA VIE DE MAURIN.

IL FAUDRA BIEN QUE JE TUE CETTE CHAROGNE UN JOUR !

MON VIEIL AMI M'OFFRIT SA MAIN ET PRESSA LA MIENNE TRÈS FORTEMENT. IL TREMBLAIT TOUT AUTANT QUE MOI ALORS QUE NOUS ATTENDIONS LE RETOUR DE MAURIN. LES OUVRIERS S'ÉTAIENT ARRÊTÉS DE TRAVAILLER. ILS ATTENDAIENT AVEC NOUS. LA FORÊT N'ÉTAIT PLUS QUE SILENCE ET FROID.

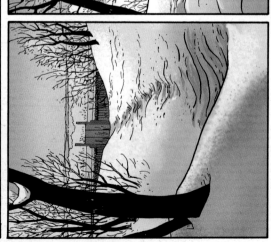

JE N'Y TIENS PLUS ! MAURIN AURAIT DÛ REVENIR DEPUIS LONGTEMPS. JE DOIS ALLER VOIR...

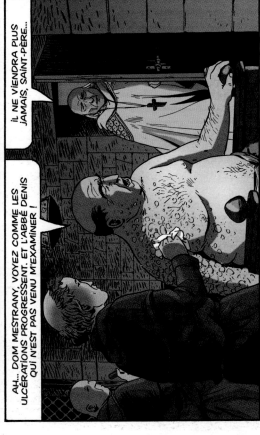

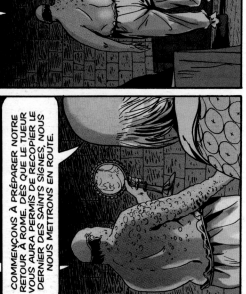

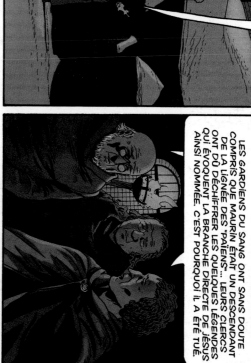

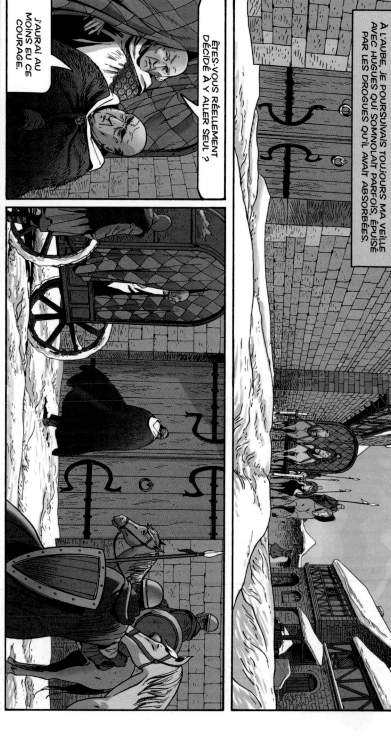

VOTRE MARI ET DE PAYNS SORTENT ENFIN DE LA CHAPELLE ?

OUI, ILS VIENNENT À LA RENCONTRE DE CET INCONNU. JE ME DEMANDE QUI IL PEUT BIEN ÊTRE ET CE QU'IL SOUHAITE... N'EST-IL PAS TROP TÔT POUR DEMANDER UNE AUDIENCE À MON ÉPOUX ?

DEMANDEZ ET JE VOUS LE DONNERAI.

JE MÉRITE VOTRE HAINE ET VOTRE CHÂTIMENT, SEIGNEUR DE PAYNS. VOUS AVEZ PERDU VOTRE FAMILLE DANS CETTE GUERRE ALORS QUE J'Y AI PERDU MON ÂME, CE QUI EST BIEN PEU ! MAIS JE VOUS ASSURE QUE JE SUIS VENU PARLER DE PAIX.

JE VOUS CROIRAI SI VOUS CONSENTEZ À ME DONNER UN GAGE DE VOTRE BONNE FOI.

JE M'AGENOUILLE À VOS PIEDS COMME UN PÉNITENT, MESSIRES. JE RENONCE À M'OPPOSER À VOUS. JE FAIS ACTE D'ALLÉGEANCE ET DE CONTRITION. DÉSORMAIS, L'ÉGLISE NE VOUS TOURMENTERA PLUS...

C'EST INCROYABLE ! DE PAYNS L'A GIFLÉ ET CET HOMME N'A PAS RÉAGI...

AU CONTRAIRE, IL ÉTEND LES BRAS EN SIGNE DE REPENTANCE. SERAIT-IL POSSIBLE QUE CE SOIT... LE PAPE ?!

38

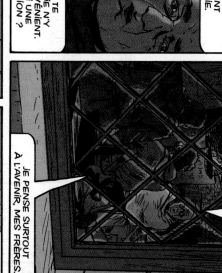

AH, SAINT-PÈRE ! J'ÉTAIS SI INQUIET... JE NE VOULAIS PAS CROIRE QUE VOUS AVIEZ QUITTÉ LE PALAIS PAR CE TEMPS ET EN PLEINE NUIT ! CELA NE ME REGARDE PAS, BIEN SÛR, CEPENDANT, JE...

CELA NE VOUS REGARDE PAS, EN EFFET, L'ÉVÊQUE.

NATURELLEMENT, C'EST LUI.

ATTENDEZ ! SI JAMAIS C'ÉTAIT LUI ?

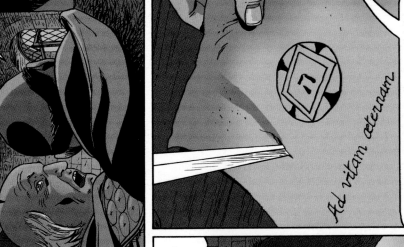

POUR LA VIE ÉTERNELLE... CE DÉMON NE MANQUE PAS DE CYNISME.

Ad vitam æternam.

VOUS RENONCEZ DONC, PÈRE ?

JE ME SUIS ACCORDÉ AVEC LES CHAMPENOIS. ILS NE RÉVÉLERONT PAS LE SECRET DE JÉSUS TANT QUE L'ÉGLISE LES LAISSERA EN PAIX. J'ESPÈRE QUE MES SUCCESSEURS MAINTIENDRONT CETTE ALLIANCE ET N'ÉCOUTERONT PAS TROP LES GARDIENS DU SANG.

MAIS IL GÈLE, ICI !

UN COURANT D'AIR VIENT DU BUREAU. QUELQU'UN A OUVERT LA FENÊTRE.

IL NE M'A PAS ATTENDU. REGARDEZ, DOM MESTRANY... IL A RECOPIÉ LUI-MÊME LE DERNIER SIGNE, ET IL A RAJOUTÉ UNE PHRASE.

IL S'EST INTRODUIT CHEZ MOI COMME À SON ORDINAIRE, PAREIL AU DAMNÉ CHAT DE SABBAT QU'IL EST...

40

OUI... OUI... JE COMPRENDS...

NOTRE MONDE NE TIENDRA QUE PAR CE FRAGILE ÉQUILIBRE, LES HOMMES ONT BESOIN DE CROIRE, ILS N'ACCEPTERAIENT PAS L'ÉPOUVANTABLE FATALITÉ DE LA MORT S'IL N'Y AVAIT PAS DE DIEU, S'IL N'Y AVAIT PLUS D'ESPOIR !

L'ENSEIGNEMENT DU CHRIST RESSUSCITÉ, UNE BELLE FOI EN LUI, NOTRE FOI CHEVILLÉE AU CORPS, SIMPLE ET ÉVIDENTE, BIEN LOIN DE LA MIENNE, CORROMPUE PAR LES CALCULS, LES PLANS, LA POLITIQUE !

J'ENVIE VOTRE FOI, DOM MESTRANY.

CETTE FIOLE ?

AH, CELA ? C'EST L'ANTIDOTE QUE M'A DONNÉ LE CHEVALIER DE PAYNS. JE DEVRAIS ÊTRE GUÉRI DANS MOINS D'UNE SEMAINE.

ET VOUS, QUE LUI AVEZ-VOUS DONNÉ EN ÉCHANGE ?

LE PAPE PASCAL N'AVAIT PU RETENIR SES LARMES, IL AVAIT LONGUEMENT PLEURÉ SUR LE CADAVRE DE MAURIN AVANT DE S'AGENOUILLER DE NOUVEAU ET DE ME BAISER LA MAIN DROITE. SES LARMES AVAIENT COULÉ ENTRE MES DOIGTS. HUGUES ET MOI L'AVIONS ENTENDU PRIER TOUT BAS. C'ÉTAIT À DIEU QU'IL DEMANDAIT PARDON.

MA FOI... C'EST BEAUCOUP D'HONNEUR POUR UN MODESTE MOINE QUE DE LIRE UNE LETTRE DU PAPE !...

RECONNAISSEZ-VOUS CE SCEAU ? C'EST CELUI DU PAPE PASCAL. LISEZ LE MESSAGE ET OBÉISSEZ À SON ORDRE.

C'EST DIEU QUI LE JUGERAIT.

VOUS LE TROUVEREZ DANS LA CHAPELLE. IL A PRIS SON BAGAGE ET SE PRÉPARE À NOUS QUITTER. IL NOUS A DIT QU'AVANT, IL SOUHAITAIT QU'ON LE LAISSE PRIER.

DÉCIDÉMENT, TU AURAS ÉTÉ BIEN MALCHANCEUX DANS CETTE AFFAIRE, CHEVALIER. TU ME FAIS PITIÉ. JE PENSERAI ET PRIERAI POUR TOI LORSQUE JE T'AURAI TUÉ.

J'AI FAIT UNE PROMESSE À MON FILS, CELLE DE TE TRANSPERCER LA POITRINE DE MON ÉPÉE.

... AVEC UN MONSTRE TEL QUE TOI !

TU ES VENU ME TUER ! ET ME REPRENDRE LES SAINTS SIGNES. TU ARRIVES TROP TARD, JE LES AI CONFIÉS À L'UN DE MES HOMMES QUI EST DÉJÀ EN ROUTE POUR ROME.

C'EST CE QU'IL AURA FAIT DE MEILLEUR DANS SA VIE ! IL A RÉALISÉ TOUTE L'HORREUR DE SON ALLIANCE AVEC LES GARDIENS DU SANG...

DE PAYNS ! LE PAPE M'A DONC TRAHI...

NE TE MORI, NE TE CORPUS*.

L'ÂME DE MON FILS NE SERA EN PAIX QUE LORSQUE TU AURAS QUITTÉ CETTE TERRE.

* NE CRAIGNEZ POINT DE MOURIR ET DE MORTIFIER VOTRE CHAIR.

À QUI PENSES-TU DE PAYNS ? À TES FRÈRES, À TON FILS ? OU BIEN À TA FEMME ET TA FILLE ? POUR QUI ÉPROUVES-TU LE PLUS DE DOULEUR ?

EH BIEN QU'IL EN FINISSE AU PLUS VITE, S'IL FAUT QUE LES AFFAIRES DU PAPE SE RÈGLENT PAR LES ARMES ! QUE NOTRE COMMUNAUTÉ RETROUVE RAPIDEMENT SON CALME !

ON SE BAT LÀ-DEDANS ! DANS NOTRE CHAPELLE !

UN CHEVALIER MANDATÉ PAR LE PAPE A DEMANDÉ À VOIR NOTRE HÔTE... MAIS PAR MA FOI, JE N'AURAIS JAMAIS CRU QUE C'ÉTAIT POUR L'ASSASSINER !

AU NOM DE MES FRÈRES !

DAMNÉ BRETTEUR...

AU NOM DE MA FAMILLE !

JUSTE UN PEU DE SANG...

TA RÉPUTATION N'ÉTAIT PAS UNE FABLE !

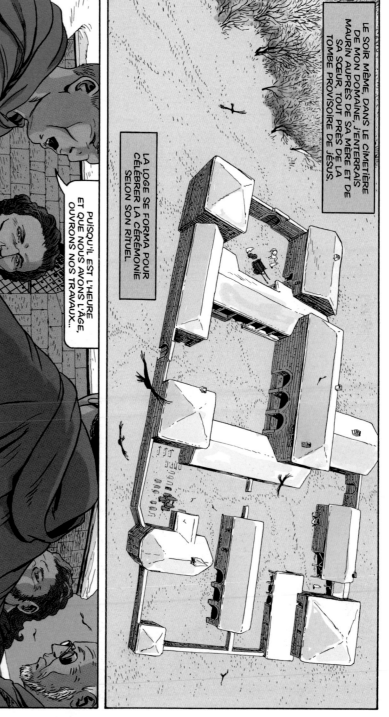

LE CONCLAVE, DOUZE JOURS APRÈS LE DÉCÈS DU PAPE JEAN, N'A TOUJOURS PAS PU SE RÉUNIR, DU FAIT DE L'HOSPITALISATION DU CARDINAL MONTESPA SAUVAGEMENT AGRESSÉ DANS LES JARDINS DU VATICAN PAR UN INCONNU QUI LUI A TRANCHÉ LA MAIN DROITE...

NOUS AVONS INVITÉ LE PROFESSEUR MONDOVI QUI VIENT DE FAIRE UN ÉTRANGE RAPPROCHEMENT ENTRE L'AGRESSION DE MONSEIGNEUR MONTESPA ET CELLE DU COMTE HUGUES DE CHAMPAGNE SURVENUE EN FRANCE AU DÉBUT DU 12E SIÈCLE... POUVEZ-VOUS NOUS EN DIRE PLUS, PROFESSEUR ?

PRÉCISONS QUE LE COMTE HUGUES DE CHAMPAGNE JOUA UN RÔLE IMPORTANT DANS LA FONDATION DE L'ORDRE DES TEMPLIERS QUE L'ON ATTRIBUE À HUGUES DE PAYNS. AVEC TROIS COMPAGNONS, TOUS CHAMPENOIS, LES DEUX HOMMES FIRENT UN PREMIER VOYAGE EN TERRE SAINTE VERS 1104. UNE EXPÉDITION SECRÈTE DONT ON N'A RETENU QUE TRÈS PEU D'INFORMATIONS.

ON SAIT SEULEMENT QUE QUELQUES ANNÉES APRÈS CETTE MYSTÉRIEUSE EXPÉDITION, LES CHEVALIERS, À L'EXCEPTION D'HUGUES DE PAYNS, EURENT TOUS LA MAIN DROITE TRANCHÉE PAR UN TUEUR MYSTÉRIEUX. TROIS D'ENTRE EUX EN MOURURENT...

DE QUELLES PREUVES DISPOSEZ-VOUS POUR ÉTAYER CETTE AFFIRMATION, PROFESSEUR ?

C'EST EN EFFET BIEN ÉTRANGE ! MAIS DE LÀ À PENSER QUE LE CARDINAL MONTESPA A ÉTÉ LA VICTIME D'UN ASSASSIN QUI A RECOPIÉ UNE SÉRIE DE CRIMES VIEUX DE DIX SIÈCLES !... ET DANS QUEL BUT ?

ENFIN !

48

CONSTANCE Y ÉVOQUE L'ATTAQUE DONT FUT VICTIME SON MARI... JE LA CITE : « J'AI BIEN CRU PERDRE MON ÉPOUX QUI PLEURAIT ENCORE LA MORT DE TROIS DE SES FIDÈLES AMIS AUXQUELS, TOUT COMME À LUI, ON A ARRACHÉ LA MAIN DROITE, SEUL LE SEIGNEUR DE PAYNS A ÉCHAPPÉ À LA MALÉDICTION DU TUEUR QU'IL A D'AILLEURS OCCIS ET RENDU AU DIABLE... »

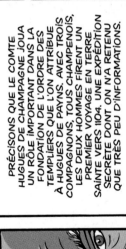

UNE LETTRE ! UN COURRIER DE CONSTANCE, L'ÉPOUSE DU COMTE DE CHAMPAGNE, QUI ÉCRIT À SON PÈRE LE ROI DE FRANCE... LE DOCUMENT, DONT VOICI LE FAC-SIMILÉ, EST ACTUELLEMENT DÉTENU PAR LA FONDATION HARDING DE LONDRES.

LES MILLIONS DE CATHOLIQUES À TRAVERS LE MONDE ATTENDENT DONC AVEC IMPATIENCE QUE LE CARDINAL MONTESPA PUISSE ENFIN SORTIR DE L'HÔPITAL POUR PARTICIPER AUX ÉLECTIONS QUI DOIVENT SE TENIR AVANT LE DIX-HUITIÈME JOUR SUIVANT L'INHUMATION DU SAINT-PÈRE, TEL QUE L'IMPOSE LA COUTUME. RAPPELONS QUE LE CARDINAL MONTESPA EST TRÈS SOUVENT CITÉ POUR COIFFER LA TIARE DE SAINT PIERRE.

MACCHI, VENEZ ! IL FAUT QUE VOUS VOYIEZ CELA À TOUT PRIX, MAINTENANT ! LE CORPS... IL...

JE... J'ARRIVE, VOUS M'AVEZ FICHU UNE SACRÉE PEUR EN DÉBOULANT DE LA SORTE. À QUOI DOIS-JE ENCORE ME PRÉPARER ?

JE SERAI SEUL ! DITES-MOI COMMENT PROCÉDER... OUI, J'ÉCOUTE... BIEN...

NATURELLEMENT QUE JE SERAI SEUL... ET ILS LE SAVENT BIEN, SI LA POLICE VENAIT FOURRER SON NEZ DANS CETTE AFFAIRE, ELLE REMONTERAIT JUSQU'À MONTESPA...

...JUSQU'AUX MEURTRES DU PROFESSEUR MOSÈLE, DE FRANCIS MARLANE ET DE TOUS LEURS AMIS, LES FRANCS-MAÇONS !*

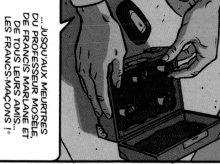

LE VATICAN NE SE RELÈVERAIT PAS D'UN TEL SCANDALE.

ELLE S'ENNUIE JUSTE UN PEU, ELLE VOUS SERA RENDUE SAINE ET SAUVE SI VOUS JOUEZ LE JEU EN VOUS CONFORMANT PRÉCISÉMENT À NOS RÈGLES. NOUS AVONS LAISSÉ PASSER DU TEMPS POUR JUGER DE VOTRE DISCRÉTION.

NOUS ALLONS VOUS DONNER L'ADRESSE OÙ VOUS RENDRE ET L'HEURE À LAQUELLE VOUS NOUS REMETTREZ LES BAGUES, MAIS VOUS DEVEZ NOUS JURER QUE VOUS NE PRÉVIENDREZ PAS LA POLICE, LA VIE DE VOTRE NIÈCE EN SERAIT COMPROMISE !

OUI, OUI... JE DÉSESPÉRAIS DE VOUS ENTENDRE ! MA NIÈCE, COMMENT SE PORTE-T-ELLE ?

OUI, J'AI LES QUATRE BAGUES... DEPUIS PLUS D'UNE SEMAINE DÉJÀ ! MAIS, ET MA NIÈCE SUZANNA ?

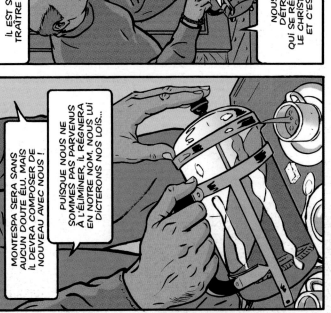

15 MINUTES À PARTIR DE MAINTENANT. PRÊTS ?...

PRÊTS !

QUATRE GRAMMES DE TARTRATE DE ZOLPIDEM ! EFFET IMMÉDIAT. DE QUOI DORMIR POUR DES HEURES.

14 MINUTES !

MAIS... QU'EST-CE QUE...?!

LE 58... C'EST ICI.

EN CELLE DE BASILE LE HARNAIS !

EN MÉMOIRE D'ARCIS DE BRIENNE !

ET EN MÉMOIRE DE GEOFFROY DE SAINT-OMER, DE MAURIN DE PAYNS AINSI QUE DE TOUS LES FRÈRES TUÉS AU COURS DES SIÈCLES PAR LES GARDIENS DU SANG !

JE... JE N'Y SUIS POUR RIEN ! JE VOUS ASSURE !!

LE SALAUD NOUS A TENDU UN PIÈGE !

MAIS...!!!

ELLE SERA DANS VOS BRAS DANS MOINS D'UNE MINUTE, DÈS QUE NOUS AURONS JETÉ UN ŒIL DANS VOTRE PORTE-DOCUMENTS. NOUS AVONS APPRIS À NOUS MÉFIER AUSSI DES HOMMES D'ÉGLISE.

TROIS COUPS SÉPARÉS PLUS UN, C'EST LUI. JE LUI OUVRE. ENFILEZ VITE VOTRE CAGOULE !

NE SOYEZ PAS SI IMPATIENT, JE VOUS AI DIT QUE JE VOUS APPORTAIS LES BAGUES. J'AI TENU MON ENGAGEMENT. OÙ EST MA NIÈCE ?

ENTREZ, MACCHI, VOTRE SERVIETTE...

ALARM

TCHOC

UNE ATTAQUE ! L'ALARME, VITE... PRESSEZ L'ALARME !

BLAM

PLUS QUE 11 MINUTES... IL NOUS EN FAUT AU MOINS SEPT POUR TRANSFÉRER LE CORPS DANS LE CAISSON ! COMMENÇONS PAR L'OXYGÈNE...

TCHOC

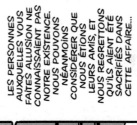

LES PERSONNES AUXQUELLES VOUS FAÎTES ALLUSION NE CONNAISSAIENT PAS NOTRE EXISTENCE. NOUS POUVONS NÉANMOINS CONSIDÉRER QUE NOUS ÉTIONS LEURS AMIS, ET NOUS REGRETTONS QU'ILS AIENT ÉTÉ SACRIFIÉS DANS CETTE AFFAIRE...

DES AMIS DE DIDIER MOSÈLE OU DE MARTIN HERTZ ? C'EST BIEN CELA ?

VOILÀ NOUS SOMMES VENUS RÉCUPÉRER LES BAGUES QUE VOUS VOUS APPRÊTIEZ À DONNER À CES HOMMES. VEUILLEZ NOUS LES RESTITUER, PROFESSEUR.

EN EFFET, NOUS NE SOMMES PAS DE LA POLICE, MAIS NOUS VOUS SURVEILLONS DEPUIS LONGTEMPS, PROFESSEUR MACCHI. VOUS, MONTESPA, LENVOISE...

COMMENT AVEZ-VOUS SU ? QUI ÊTES-VOUS ? VOUS N'ÊTES PAS DE LA POLICE, N'EST-CE PAS ?...

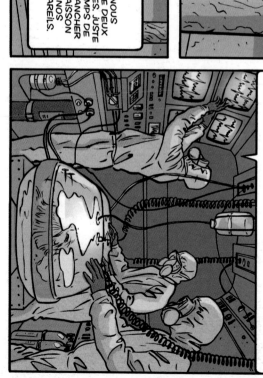

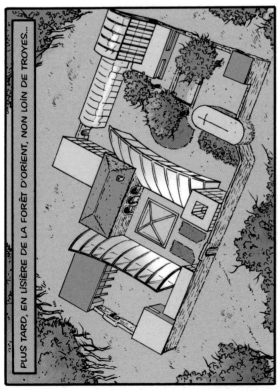

FIN

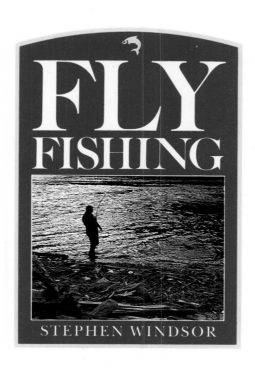

FLY FISHING

STEPHEN WINDSOR

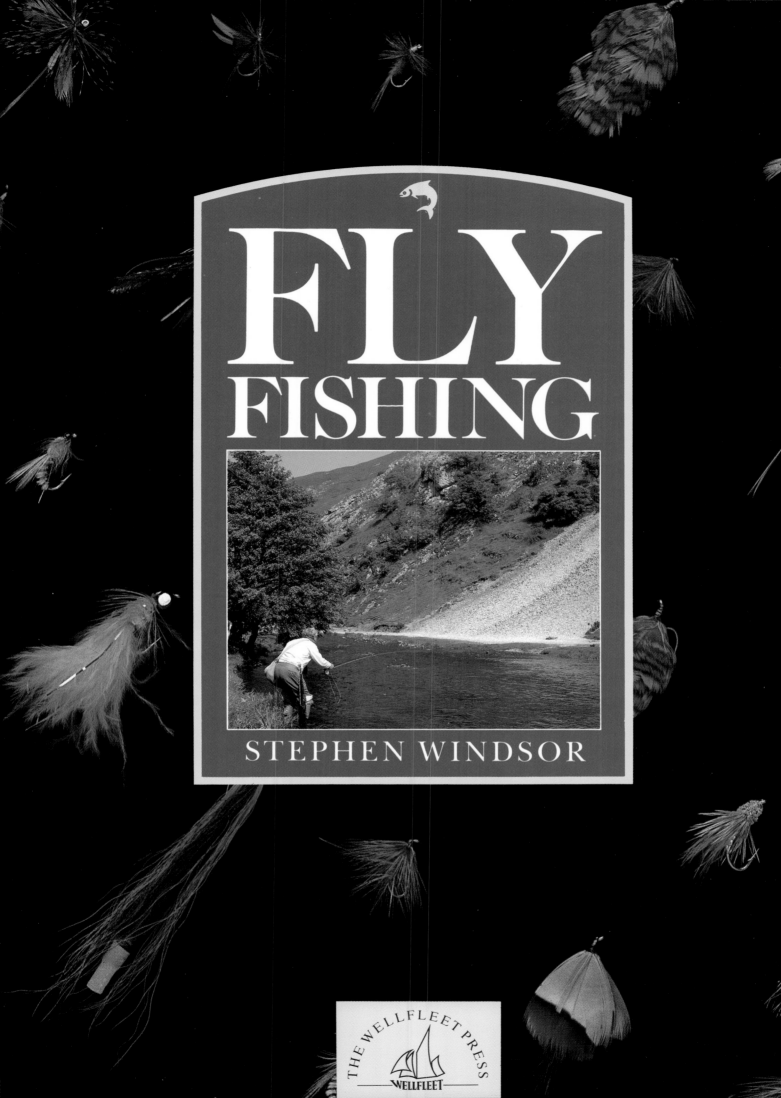

FLY FISHING

STEPHEN WINDSOR

THE WELLFLEET PRESS
WELLFLEET

For Gerd, patient fishing widow, and for Hannah and
Magnus: may there still be pure water and fish for them
to catch.

A QUINTET BOOK

Published by Wellfleet Press
110 Enterprise Avenue
Secaucus, New Jersey 07094

ISBN 1-55521-400-2

This book was designed and produced by
Quintet Publishing Limited
6 Blundell Street
London N7 9BH

Art Director: Peter Bridgewater
Designer: Ian Hunt
Editors: Len Cacutt, Judith Simons
Additional photography: Andrew Sydenham
Illustrator: Paul Crawford

Typeset in Great Britian by
Central Southern Typesetters, Eastbourne
Manufactured in Hong Kong by
Regent Publishing Services Limited
Printed in Hong Kong by
South Sea Int'l Press Ltd.

ACKNOWLEDGEMENTS
The author and publisher would like to extend their
thanks to The Orvis® Co. Inc., Stockbridge, England,
and Manchester, USA, for providing the photographs for
Chapter 8, and C. Farlowe and Co Ltd., London, for
providing tackle and equipment for photography. The
author would also like to thank the following who
knowingly or unknowingly have helped in the writing
of this book: Peter Gathercole, Gordon Fraser, Steve
Parton, Bev Perkins, Charles Jardine, Chris Dawn and
John Wilshaw.

CONTENTS

INTRODUCTION 6

FLY FISHING TACKLE 8

PUTTING IT ALL TOGETHER 18

THE FLY FISHERMAN'S FISH 26

THE WATERS WE FISH 36

FLIES AND FLY LIFE 54

THE FLY FISHERMAN'S TACTICS & TECHNIQUES 72

FLY DRESSING 98

POPULAR FLY PATTERNS 108

BIBLIOGRAPHY 125

INDEX 126

INTRODUCTION

". . . be quiet; and go a' Angling."
IZAAK WALTON, 'COMPLEAT ANGLER'.

*T*O be a fly fisherman is both a joy and an affliction. Few more testing yet delightful ways of catching a fish exist, and no one would choose to hunt their food in such a way if survival was their main obsession. There are many easier ways to catch fish, especially a creature as cussed as a salmon or downright dumb as a trout. Fly casting is an efficient way to get a bait to a fish. Flies, imitative, or even designed to infuriate are an unlikely way to simulate a living creature when the living creature could often be impaled on a hook, and cast with fine monofilament and a reel after a few minutes tuition.

The fly fisherman can trace his roots to a very different age, when the long whip-like rod and tapered line would be the only way to flick out a fly. His method should long ago have been superseded, instead it thrives and grows, with ever more converts to the sport becoming entranced with its pleasures. Fly fishing is not merely a sport, it is an art, one in which keenness of eye and control of hand are vital. The fly-fisherman's canvas is the water, his critics are the trout, and his rewards blessedly tangible. For the rise, the take, the pull and the battle of the trout, salmon, or any sporting fish are all more pleasureable when fly tackle is used than with almost any other fishing method.

It is a year-round pursuit too, and not just because so many different species may fall to the lure of a fly. Tackle care and, more to the point, flydressing and the study of entomology become essential parts of the full enjoyment of the sport. Winter evenings indoors are never dull, there is always work for idle hands, and even the least dexterous can produce wisps of fur and feather that will deceive the craftiest trout.

At first, the skills are easily mastered, but the full lesson is never learnt. Trout, salmon and lunker pike make no differentiation between novice and expert. The well-presented fly conquers all, and if at first that presentation lacks finesse, there will be younger, less tutored, perhaps downright stupid fish to oblige.

The following chapters open the doors to the kindergarten class, but the full lesson will take a pleasurable lifetime by the water, and yet never be fully learnt.

Dry fly on the River Lambourn, southern England. The angler is in pursuit of grayling – the Lady of the Stream.

CHAPTER ONE

FLY FISHING TACKLE

*F*LY fishing differs from all other forms of angling in that the line provides the casting weight. It is the secret of presenting a tiny, near weightless fly, to a fish at distances of up to 50yd (46m).

To get this method of casting to work at its best great casting skills are necessary (to be discussed later), but balanced tackle is also required. What is meant by balanced? All fly rods and fly lines are rated by AFTMA numbers so that they can be perfectly matched for casting performance. A #7 rod will work with a #7 line, although it is not quite as simple as that, because the rod will in fact work with the first 30ft (9m) of that #7 line.

Lines are available from about a #3 up to a #13. Of course, there are rods to match, and some of them will not be graded for just one line but two, perhaps even three. So you might see a #7–to–#8 rod, but with the superb graphite rods available these days this need not concern the beginner. As a novice, err to the heavier side and choose an #8 line. The question of which weight and length of rod, matched to which weight of line, is needed to catch fish with a fly will be discussed shortly.

First, though, let's take a look in turn at rods, and lines, and try to establish just what you need to look for when buying them.

RODS

Rods are available in three main materials – glassfibre, graphite (carbon fibre), or bamboo (split-cane). Graphite is the best material currently available for the vast majority of fly rods, so the others can be disposed of quickly.

Glassfibre is now refined to perfection. Rods in this material are durable, slightly heavier than graphite, and generally less stiff. Consequently you need a broader cross-section on a glass rod, and even then it will lack the accuracy and crispness of graphite. However, it is an excellent material for slow-actioned shorter rods, and quite nice for heavy-duty ocean fly fishing. Bamboo is constructed from split sections of bamboo, glued and joined to form a six-sided rod. Building such weapons is craftsman's work, and the finished item is a thing of beauty. Split-cane, far heavier than man-made fibres, is very accurate due to its flat-sided construction, and a

The three main materials used for fly-fishing rods are (right) glassfibre, (left) graphite (carbon fibre) and (middle) bamboo (splitcane).

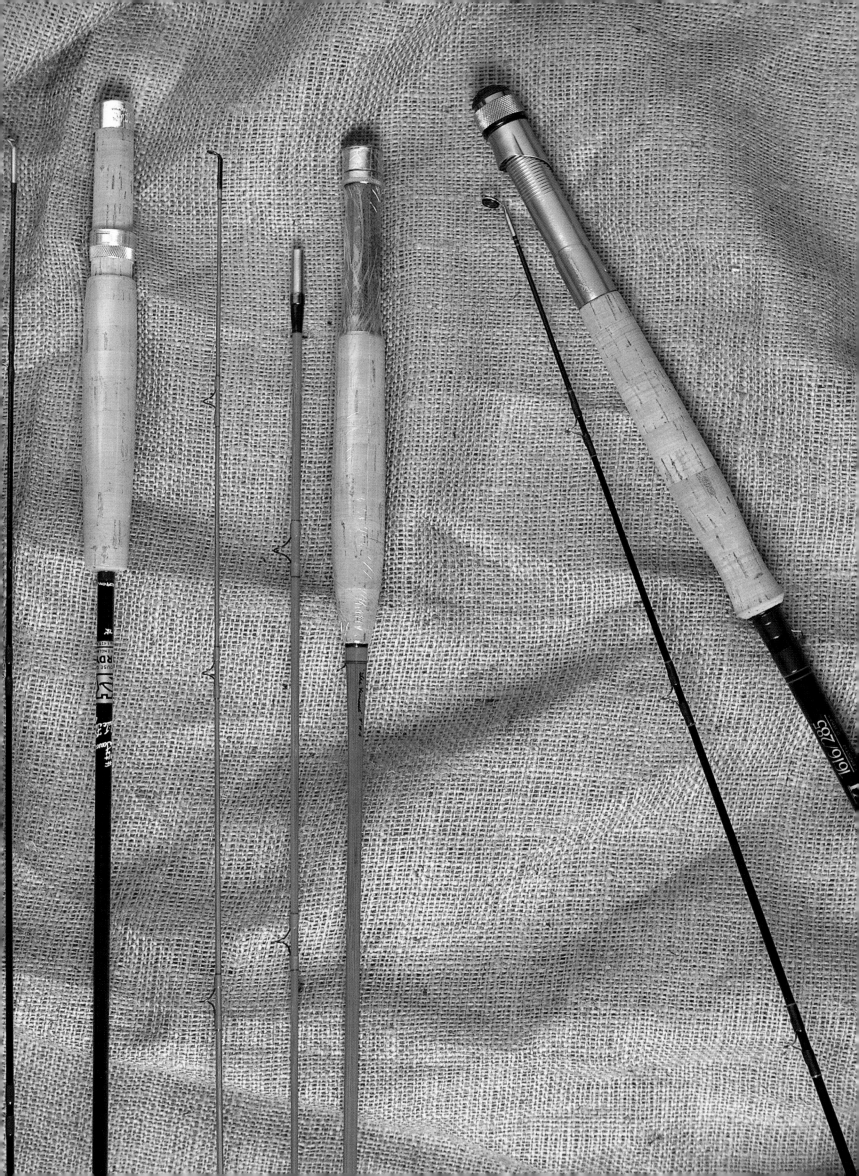

joy to fish with on small streams. It also handles fish well, and sets hooks home soundly. But over 8ft (2.5m) it becomes cumbersome – and is very expensive. So, for everyday fishing, graphite has to be the choice. In the ten or so years it has been available it has revolutionized fly rod construction; light and durable unless hit hard from the side, with intelligent rod design it can be supplied with almost any conceivable action.

At the bottom of the rod, there will be a reel seat, preferably one that tucks the reel up under the hand rather than leaving it wobbling at the bottom of the rod, and a handle, which will generally be of cork. It would be nice if rod handles were left unfinished so that the angler could shape them to his own design. Sadly this is not the case, and it is advisable to try several different shapes to find the one that suits you.

Your rod will have guides – rod rings – of one of two sorts. The first is the classic snake guide. Made of wire, it is light, flexible, and these days usually of durable and corrosion-proof metal. These rings are highly recommended, except in areas where they will be subjected to constant wear through double-hauling (described in Chapter 2) or if used on a gritty bank, when the second type of ring, a more solid type with a 'liner' of very hard material such as silicone carbide, is preferable. There are two minor drawbacks to this type of ring; they create a lot of friction on the line when casting, which will reduce distance, and they are heavier and less flexible than snake rings. To compensate, they virtually never need changing.

ABOVE *Guides (rod rings) for the modern rod; snake rings (top) and hard-lined Fuji's (below).*

Rods are available in lengths from 5ft (1.5m) to the British salmon rod of up to 20ft (6m). However, the vast majority of normal fly fishing will be done with rods from 8 to 10ft (2.5–3m), with 9ft (2.7m) being a useful compromise and all-round length. Few long-distance tournament casters feel the need for a rod longer than 10ft (3m), and rod length has little effect on casting distance when compared with choice and profile of line.

Later we will describe five basic outfits for all fly fishing – but following these guidelines the beginner will be well-equipped for small to quite large rivers, and most still-waters, with a carbon rod of 9–9½ft (2.7–2.9m) long, equipped with snake guides, and possibly a silicone carbide or similar ring at the butt to take the added stress and friction of casting. This rod will be rated for a particular weight of fly line. Which weight is a good compromise for the novice armed with this rod, will be discussed shortly, but first, to clarify

the choice of line weights, and indeed of any fly line, an explanation of the fly line itself is needed.

FLY LINES

PROFILES AND SINKING RATES
Modern fly lines are constructed with a plastic coat of PVC over a Terylene core. The plastic can be distributed on to the core in a taper so that it results in a line 'profile'. However, 'modern' is a relative term. Twenty years ago fly lines were commonly made of silk, but now PVC line has taken over completely – which is not to say that it is the ultimate fly line. Time will tell if the new polymer coating on the Kevlar-core fly lines will live up to their manufacturer's many promises, and replace the old-style line. My feeling is that, like silk, the old PVC line will survive for many years, since it has some advantages over the new lines.

Back to basics – what profiles do the manufacturers build into their fly lines? There are two basic types, double-taper (which as the name suggests has a taper at each end), and forward-taper or weight-forward (where instead of a line with an even taper at both ends, the main casting weight is at the front end). Now (as you have read), the first 30ft (9m) of the line supplies the correct casting weight for the rod. So a gently tapering 30ft (9m) of double-taper (and in practice some level centre section) will weight a matched rod, and must be moved through the air to cast.

On a forward-taper, however, the casting weight in the form of that belly is pushed up nearer the front of the line, and in aerializing 30ft (9m) of line, you are not only

making the rod work perfectly, but also getting all of the 'thick bit' of the line outside the tip ring of the rod. Now, by single or double-hauling to get more line speed (see Chapter 2), you can cast out this belly, with nothing but the resistance of fine running-line or back taper to slow your cast.

Try the same with a double-taper line, and you have a lot of thick belly line resisting your efforts. So why bother with a double-taper line at all? Well, apart from the obvious benefit that you can reverse the line and use the other end when one end wears out, a double-taper line used for short casts can present a fly far more delicately than a forward-taper, which has a more gradual taper from a fine tip. It is also more accurate.

SHOOTING-HEADS

The logical development therefore is the shooting-head. Why not cut off the first 30ft (9m) of a double-taper and smoothly join it to fine running line (usually monofilament such as 30lb (13.5kg) Stren)? That 30ft (9m) can then be cast further, without losing the fine tip and presentation. Now take the proposition even further: if it is hard work to aerialize 30ft (9m) of fly line, why not cut the shooting-head from a line one or two sizes heavier? A shorter length will still make the rod work. Perhaps 20ft (6m) of #9 fly line will work with a #7–rated rod. The resultant line is called a shooting-head and with its many variations it is the weapon for long-casting – though the principle of improved presentation relies on considerable casting skills.

So the line profile the angler

ABOVE *A selection of internationally available fly lines for the modern fisherman, including sinkers, slow sinkers, floaters and sink-tips. Most are coated with PVC, although Airflo lines are covered with a tougher polymer coating.*

chooses will depend on his venue. Small rivers and tiny ponds require double-taper lines, all short-casting situations are better met with them. Larger rivers and still-waters in general will probably call for a forward-taper. Shooting-heads are handy for all long-range work, and are used most often for big river sea-trout, steelhead, single-handed salmon fishing, and, fly fishing at sea, where long casts are often essential.

FLOATING AND SINKING LINES

Fly lines can be constructed to do everything from floating high to sinking like a stone. There are a variety of methods of achieving this, from incorporating air into the coating to adding metals, either ground-up in the coating, or in the shape of a fine lead-core to the line. However, while the technology need not concern us, the fact that a huge range of fly lines with accurately-rated sinking speeds is avail-

able, should. For instance, a line is available that will sink so slowly that it fishes just under the surface film and eliminates line wake; another will sink a foot down on the same retrieve; a third will fish 2ft (.6m) down, and so on. Fly fishermen tend to use vague terms such as fast-sinker, medium-sinker, slow-sinker, intermediate, and neutral-density, without explaining that one manufacturer's slow-sinker is another's medium, and so on.

Various sinking speeds are important for obvious reasons. One is that a very fast sinker will mean less waiting time to fish deep on a stillwater; another is that it might be the only line that will get deep enough in a fast-flowing river. There are less obvious reasons, too. Consider side-casting from a drifting boat. If your partner locates fish at a certain depth (perhaps by counting down his line), you may need exactly the same line to reach those fish. Not only that, but the same profile of line, and the same casting distance from the side of the boat. In short, carrying a range of lines helps you to cope with factors beyond your control.

The novice river angler may need no more than a floating line for 99 per cent of the time; the stillwater man is better equipped with a floater, fast-sinker, and neutral-density or intermediate in that order; the angler who fishes for salmon and steelhead may need a whole range of shooting heads. One last note on fly lines. On occasions a mixed line can pay dividends. There are commercially produced lines with a sinking-tip section of perhaps 10ft (3m), on a floating line. These have a role in still-water nymphing, and can be helpful in holding a wet fly down when casting downstream and across on rivers. They can also be homemade by joining two sections, or spare pieces of sinking line can be carried and looped on in an emergency. At the other end of the scale, and unavailable commercially, so it must be homemade, comes a float-tip line, which is sometimes handy when fishing deep in snaggy or weedy water to hold a fly up off the bottom.

WHAT WEIGHT?

The novice angler faced with lines from #3 to #13 could be forgiven for panicking. However, compromise comes in the middle of the range, and a line weight of #6 or #7 will be adequate for all but the largest and smallest waters. For heavy work and long-casting you can use a weight-forward #8, or some shooting-heads matched to the rod.

As you progress in both knowledge of fish and casting skill you may well discover the delights of light tackle. A #4 outfit is a joy to use, and because the line has less inertia and the rod less stiffness, far lighter tippets may be used.

REELS

A line needs to be loaded onto a reel and many top fly fishermen use their reels as little more than line reservoirs, playing their fish by hand and not bothering to wind loose line back onto the reel. This presupposes that the hooked fish is not going to make a long run, for if this happens they will be down

ABOVE *Some of the finest fly reels on the market, from Hardy, Scientific Anglers and the brilliant Dutch craftsman Ari Hart. The reels in the lefthand row are for smaller-stream fishing – although the System Two (second from top) has a superb brake; those in the righthand row are for big-stillwater, steelhead and sea trout fishing.*

to the line and backing stored on the reel and might as well take advantake of its facilities.

There are two main types of fly reel, single-action, or multiplying. Single-action reels retrieve one diameter's worth of line for each turn; the spool of a multiplying reel may make three or four rotations for each turn of the handle, which is handy when fish make long runs then turn and come back towards you. For small rivers, and quite a lot of stillwater fishing, single-action reels suffice, and they should be big enough to hold your fly line, plus sufficient backing to cope with any running fish you are likely to encounter. This will vary from 30yd (27m) on small rivers

and ponds to 200yd (183m) when hunting salmon, and even more when ocean fishing.

There is a valid argument for using a wide-diameter reel when fishing with a shooting-head, because such a spool puts less of a coil into the backing.

Reels are available which feature everything from a simple click drag (which is surprisingly effective at slowing down even quite large trout), to a superb braking mechanism. Every system needs to be suitable for, or sensibly adjusted to, the species of fish you are seeking and the strength of your tippet.

BACKING

Backing can either be a reservoir of stout line, usually monofilament, or more sophisticated, when used with shooting-heads. Backing is used, quite simply, because a 30-yd (27-m) fly line does not give room for manoeuvre when playing a big fish.

Shooting head backing is actually cast off the reel and because of this it should be slick and relatively tangle-free. For sinking heads use 30lb (13.5kg) Stren, or a flattened nylon backing; for floaters add grease to the nylon, or use braided backing, which casts superbly. Expensive alternatives are fly-line-style running lines, very fine, and made in floating or sinking forms.

LEADERS AND TIPPETS

At the business end of the fly line, a huge range of leaders is available, but many anglers choose to make their own. Braided leaders can be

ABOVE *Standard tapered and braided leaders, including a fast-sinking braided version.*

made up of gradually descending diameters of neatly knotted braided nylon; they are also available as a tapered weave in one piece. Such leaders can have wire woven into them, or lead wire running through their centres to make them sink. They can be sealed to float, greased to float, or have other materials incorporated into them. These leaders turn over the rest of the tippet well and add a delicate taper to the point of a fly line. They are easy to attach permanently, usually last well and can also be locked in place with a plastic sleeve and quickly changed. In their sinking versions they go a long way to making the sink-tip line redundant, but are a boon to the dry-fly angler when they float well and present the fly accurately. Their construction has a degree of stretch built in too, so there is a cushion against smash takes. All in all they seem useful in lengths up to 4 or 5ft (1–1.5m) as the back taper of a leader. In greater lengths they seem badly troubled by wind,

and are more awkward to control in the water than plain nylon. Still, the novice, especially on rivers, should try them, probably in combination with a standard tapered leader, made of tapered monofilament.

They are available with very stiff butts, and in a variety of tippet strengths, colours, and stiffnesses. The novice may make up his own tapered leaders by knotting gradually tapering lengths of nylon, and many formulas for the perfect leader are available.

Most commercially produced leaders are between 9 and 12ft (2.5–3.5m) long, and for stillwater use they need an extra length of tippet nylon knotted onto them because a longer leader usually brings more takes, or when a dropper is required. Most fly fishermen need to carry tippet nylon from 2 to 8lb (1–3.5kg) breaking strain, with heavier line for big migratory trout, salmon, northern pike, very big bass and sea fish.

A lot has been said about the colour of nylon, but a nice compromise is to match the tinge of the water: clear for clear water; pale blue in the sea; brown in brown-tinged or peaty water; green when algae tinges the water green. However, colour makes little difference if the fly is well-presented.

FLIES

The great essential for success in this sport is the right fly. Notes on choice of fly, fly dressing, and patterns, are given later, but a few guidelines need stressing. There is no point in fishing a superb fly on a

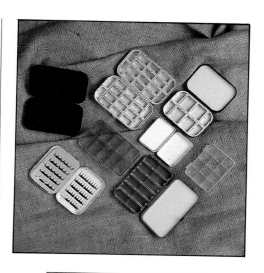

ABOVE *Fly boxes range from the simple and inexpensive to the high-priced and immaculate – each one of this range has a role to play.*

terrible hook. The point must be sharp and the temper of the wire perfect. Whether buying hooks with flies ready-tied on them, or tying them yourself, check the hook points.

Artificial flies should also be kept free from rust. Take time after each trip to dry the flies out, and protect fly boxes from rain and damp (although I remember occasions when a rust-dulled tinsel body was more acceptable than a bright flashy one!).

Learn to tie your own flies – it is essential both for economy and for ensuring that you carry sufficient patterns. If you tie your own you can match obscure hatches, ensure that you can always get hold of some more of a killing pattern and copy a friend's successful fly.

Fly boxes should be well made, with reliable closing catches, sound hinges, and should float. If they are brightly coloured, it gives them less chance of being lost. A number of pocket-sized boxes are often more useful than one suitcase-

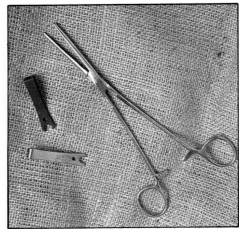

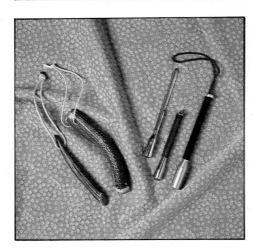

ABOVE TOP *A most useful fishing vest or waistcoat.*

ABOVE MIDDLE *Forceps are excellent hook removers and make a useful stream-side fly vice. Clippers ensure neat knots.*

ABOVE BOTTOM *Always carry a priest – perhaps incorporating a marrow spoon – to kill your fish.*

sized one – as long as the contents are clearly labelled. Dry flies, many wet flies, and some nymphs require boxes that will not crush the delicate hackles or legs.

SMALL BUT VITAL

A multi-pocketed fishing waistcoat or vest is usually more useful than a bag for holding what the fly angler needs close to hand, especially when wading. A simple belt pack system is the choice of other anglers. What goes into all those pockets? There are spare shooting-heads, spare fly reels, and reel spools loaded with lines, fly boxes, leaders, and tippet nylon. It should contain the following items, each with a role to play: artery forceps for removing hooks, line clippers with a sharp point for clearing hook eyes and unravelling knots, a weighted cosh for killing fish (called a 'priest'), and a marrow spoon for sampling the stomach contents of dead fish in order to see what it was feeding on. Carry two pairs of polarized sunglasses, a yellow pair for bad light, standard for bright light. These both protect the eyes when casting, and even more important in actual fishing, help you to see fish underwater.

You could also carry a pot of grease like Gunk, to help float the leader and, occasionally, the fly line tip; a sinking agent like Gink, to make the leader sink; a small phial of detergent to degrease your line and fingers before it migrates onto unwanted areas of your tackle; and a bottle of dry-fly proofing, for waterproofing flies.

A large back pocket can accommodate a lightweight waterproof jacket. Some vests also have clips

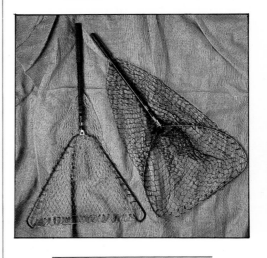

ABOVE TOP *Sunglasses both protect the eyes and in practical terms help you spot fish.*

ABOVE MIDDLE *Grease and sinking agents aid fly presentation.*

ABOVE BOTTOM *A good-sized landing net is always useful.*

for a net, if required, a rod-holding system which leaves the hands free, and a patch which holds flies securely while they dry. There is a similar band on my favourite fishing hat, and a fly patch on my peaked cap. It is a real disaster if I leave my vest at home!

CLOTHING

It is impossible to give too many guidelines on clothing as the climate and terrain where game fish are sought varies so much. I would not fly fish without a hat, preferably with a large peak to help keep excess light out from behind my fish-spotting polarized glasses. When wading it is essential to wear clothing that will remain warm when wet, and which dries quickly. Wherever possible, spare dry clothing should be carried. Buy the best waterproof outer clothing you can afford, and err towards the type of clothing preferred by other outdoor sportsmen who put their lives at the risk of the weather – mountaineers for example. Remember, too, that if it is cold on shore it will be colder in a boat on a large water, and icy when wading in the water. Take extra clothing and wear sensible long underwear – several layers are warmer than one big topcoat.

At the other extreme, protect your skin from the sun, and bear in mind that bright sun reflects from water to enhance its rays when you are in a boat or deep wading. Barrier creams, sensible hats and, if necessary, long sleeves, may be essential.

Footwear should be considered in conjunction with temperature, whether wading and whether a

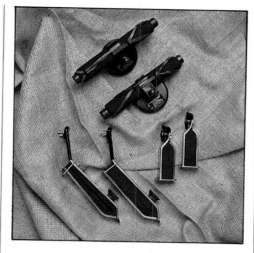

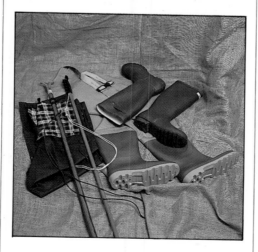

ABOVE TOP Rod holders allow you to carry made-up rods on your car.

ABOVE MIDDLE Modern or more traditional, the anglers' clothing must be functional

ABOVE BOTTOM Waterproof over-trousers and footwear are equally essential and a wading staff to probe the river bed is a necessary safety item.

slippery river or lake bed requires studs or other grips. Common sense will indicate what you will need. When deep wading, the old-fashioned buoyant wading staff with a rubber-tipped weighted end is still a most useful item.

CARE OF TACKLE

Today's graphite rods need little special care. Wipe them down occasionally and oil any metal reel seat parts. Check the guides for cracks and grooves and the varnish on the whippings. The occasional dab of varnish will keep water out of any cracks, stopping discoloration, and prevent silk whippings from rotting. You must learn how to whip-on a new rod ring. Keep fly lines and all nylon away from sources of heat and sunlight.

Fly lines benefit from an occasional wash in soft soap and a dose of replasticizer. They should also be taken off reels when not in use for a time and loosely coiled. String them out in the open air and give them a good stretch before using them again. Sunlight ruins nylon, and one professional of my acquaintance keeps his stocks in the fridge. It is sound practice to throw nylon away after a season's use, and if a spool shows any signs of poor knot strength, or experiences mysterious breaks, throw it away.

The great enemy of fly reels is grit and dirt. All you need to do is keep them clean, and well-oiled. If you are using a reel that might corrode in saltwater, rinse and dry it thoroughly after use. New reels are sometimes packed with heavy grease, and they generally run smoother if this is removed and

some good quality oil substituted. Plenty of WD40 is an effective lazy man's way to maintenance. Flies kept long in storage should be protected from moths and other bugs with a proprietary deterrent; damp fly boxes should be opened and stood over a moderate heat source to dry. If they are stuck on to anything that holds water, such as a woollen fly patch, take them out and dry both patch and flies separately.

Any kind of rubber boot or wader will benefit from storage in a cool, sun-free place, away from electrical switches. Unfold and hang them upside down by the foot. For on-the-bank repairs, nothing beats cynoacrilate glue, which as will be seen in the next chapter, securely attaches a braided leader.

KEEPING A RECORD

You will find it very handy to maintain a record of your fishing trips in a notebook, for ready reference as the seasons pass. Keep it at home, or with you on your travels. Note the weather and water conditions and the successful flies and tackle. You will also want to record the fish you catch. You might also carry a tape measure in your vest (or have one painted on your rod), and possibly a small spring balance. Best of all, carry one of today's tiny but fool-proof 35mm cameras, and record your catch for posterity and your life-long delight.

SMALL STREAMS AND PONDS
- **Quarry:** trout, grayling, panfish, small bass
- **Rod:** 6 to 7ft graphite rod #4
- **Fly line:** floating double-taper line #4 (sometimes #5 or #6 where a short cast is made and less fly line is needed to balance the rod)
- **Leaders:** 6 to 9ft (1.8–2.7m) long
- **Tippets:** up to 4lb (1.8kg)
- **Flies:** small streamers, popping bugs, wet flies, nymphs and dry flies

MEDIUM-SIZED RIVERS AND PONDS, SMALL WATERS WITH LOW VEGETATION NEEDING A HIGH BACKCAST
- **Quarry:** trout, grayling, panfish, small steelhead and sea trout
- **Rod:** 8ft (2.4m) graphite rod #5 to #6
- **Reel:** single-action or small multiplying fly reel with 50yd (46m) of backing
- **Fly line:** floating double-taper #5 for presentation; weight-forward #6 for distance; or weight-forward #6-medium and fast sinkers
- **Leaders:** 6 to 20ft (1.8–6m) long, sometimes with droppers
- **Tippets:** 2 to 6lb (1.2–7kg)
- **Flies:** small streamers, popping bugs, wet flies, nymphs and dry flies

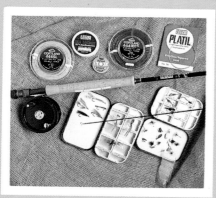

STANDARD OUTFIT – STILLWATER NYMPHING AND LARGE RIVERS

- **Quarry:** trout, grayling, bass, panfish, steelhead, sea trout, northern pike and light sea fishing
- **Rod:** 9 or 9½ft (2.7 or 2.9m) graphite #6 and #7
- **Reel:** single-action or multiplying fly reel with 100yd (91m) of backing; shooting-head backing as required
- **Fly line:** double-taper #6 floater; weight-forward #7 floater; range of sinking weight-forward or shooting-heads as required
- **Leaders:** 9 to 20ft (2.7–6m) long
- **Tippets:** 3 to 8lb (1.4–3.6kg), plus wire where required
- **Flies:** large streamers, popping bugs, full range of wet flies, nymphs and dry flies

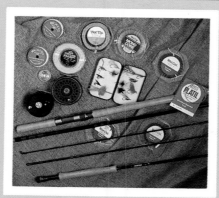

HEAVY OUTFIT – LARGE RIVERS, LAKES AND OCEAN FISHING

- **Quarry:** single-handed salmon, steelhead, sea trout, largemouth bass, northern pike and muskellunge, tarpon (small shark)
- **Rod:** 10 or 10½ft (3 or 3.2m) #8 or #9; double-handed European salmon fly rod to 16ft (5m) or more
- **Reel:** very large capacity reel – single-action may be more reliable – with a superb braking system and loaded with 200yd (183m) or more of backing; also shooting-head backing
- **Fly line:** full range of shooting-heads with various sinking speeds; salmon double-hander will require a range of heavy double-taper lines
- **Leaders:** to 20ft (6m)
- **Tippets:** 5 to 15lb (2.2–6.8kg), plus wire trace where necessary
- **Flies:** large salmon, steelhead and ocean flies, big poppers, huge bucktails for pike, and big dry flies for salmon

CLASSIC LOCH-STYLE OUTFIT – BOAT FISHING ON BIG LOCHS, LOUGHS AND LAKES

This last outfit is included as a curiosity, but the method it encompasses is a classic one that has stood the test of time.

- **Quarry:** trout, sea trout, salmon
- **Rod:** 11 or 12ft (3.3 or 3.6m) graphite rod, slow-actioned, for #5 or #6
- **Reel:** single-action or multiplying reel; backing depends on species encountered – up to 150yd (137m) for salmon
- **Fly line:** double-taper #5 floater or #6 floater for traditional-style short casting; similar # intermediate line can be useful
- **Leaders:** 12 to 20ft (3.6–6m) long with two or three droppers
- **Tippets:** 2 to 6lb (1–2.7kg)
- **Flies:** classic wet fly selection with plenty of palmered top-dropper flies; small standard Atlantic salmon and sea trout lures; tiny muddlers (for top droppers, dressed on standard wet fly 10s and smaller); range of stillwater nymphs where suitable

PUTTING IT ALL TOGETHER

NOT a few aspiring fly fisher-men have arrived at the water's edge, raring to go, only to discover that their newly acquired and much-loved fishing tackle has no intention of allowing them to cast or even to begin to fish properly. Perhaps when they do hook a fish they find it impossible to play, a jammed reel or poor knots causing them the ultimate irritation to a novice — the loss of that all-important first trout of their fly-fishing careers.

It is not enough to have the best tackle and even to employ it brilliantly if a simple item such as a knot, or the balance of your tackle, lets you down. The importance of balanced tackle has been stressed in Chapter 1 — for good casting, balanced tackle is everything. But having acquired an immaculate rod-and-line combination and carefully not crippled it with a too-heavy reel and an understrength leader, and not having tried to use the outfit on rivers or lakes where it is too powerful, we must assemble it all. Unlike other branches of the sport of angling, the fly fisherman will benefit from spending some time at home first putting his outfit together. There are quick

methods of assembling fly fishing tackle at the waterside but they are untrustworthy.

The novice may prefer to put his trust in the tried and tested knots, not the new-fangled glues and tubes, but these modern methods are worth a look. Before we consider them we should introduce rod to reel. You may prefer to fish with your reel set up for left- or right-handed use, and the majority of reels on the market allow both functions. So decide and set the reel as necessary; it may mean turning a switch or merely moving a cog with a screw-driver. Whatever the method it is rarely a taxing job.

Depending on where you are planning to fish you will most probably want to put some backing on your reel, anything from 32 to 220yd (30–200m) as advised in Chapter 1. Wind this on under gentle tension, and distribute the line with your fingers as you wind, so that the backing forms a smooth and level basis for the fly line. Hollow backing will now be attached to the fly line by sliding the line up the backing and fixing it in place with a cynoacrilate glue. Whip over the join with fly tying

Roll casting with the long salmon rod on Scotland's River Lyon.

silk to smooth the edge. Probably the safest knot to join flat nylon or standard monofilament line to the fly line is the needle knot (*see* diagram). Soft backings like Terylene can be tied on with the nail knot, though it is advisable to put a single half-hitch in the fly line before tying the nail knot (*see* diagram). Alternatively you may prefer to use glue.

It has been my experience that all cynoacrilate joins should be checked regularly because they break down very quickly in water.

Now wind on the fly line following the manufacturer's instructions. If they are lost or there were none, place the coiled fly line over a rolled-up magazine, cut any packing tyings, or untwist any wires, and unwind the line ensuring that it has no twists. These will cause unbelievable problems at a later date if they find their way onto your reel. Infuriatingly, there is no certain way of getting just enough backing and fly line to fill any particular reel at the first attempt. Again, follow the manufacturer's instructions as to capacity. Do not attempt to fish with an overfull reel, it will damage the line and make the playing of trout very difficult.

Now for the leader. As was discussed in Chapter 1, there is now a huge range of leaders available on the market, and 90 per cent of these have much to commend them. Let us discuss their attachment to the business end of the line.

Generally of braided nylon, the best hollow leaders are tapered down in one length, others are joined with knots in tapered stages. Either way they are simple to

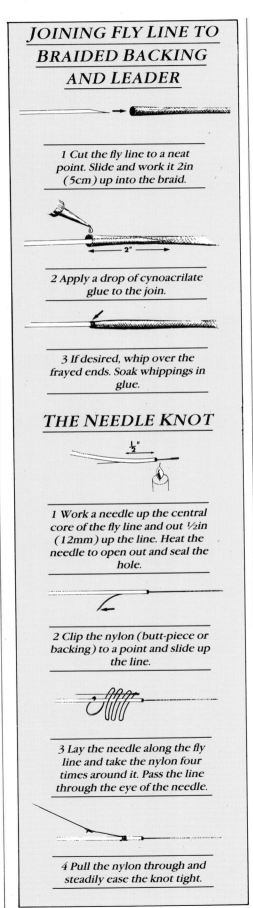

JOINING FLY LINE TO BRAIDED BACKING AND LEADER

1 Cut the fly line to a neat point. Slide and work it 2in (5cm) up into the braid.

2 Apply a drop of cynoacrilate glue to the join.

3 If desired, whip over the frayed ends. Soak whippings in glue.

THE NEEDLE KNOT

1 Work a needle up the central core of the fly line and out ½in (12mm) up the line. Heat the needle to open out and seal the hole.

2 Clip the nylon (butt-piece or backing) to a point and slide up the line.

3 Lay the needle along the fly line and take the nylon four times around it. Pass the line through the eye of the needle.

4 Pull the nylon through and steadily ease the knot tight.

attach to the fly line. The tip, which may be cut to a point, is simply threaded up inside the braid. Once there, it can be glued and overwhipped right at the end. Provided at least 16in (4cm) are slid over the fly line, a dab of glue should suffice.

To employ the useful quick-change facility of the leaders, some manufacturers offer tubes of thin plastic which lock the leaders in place, but can quickly be removed should a sinking leader be needed in place of a floater. These links are usually trustworthy, but many old hands distrust anything but a knot they have tied themselves!

Twisted leaders, the precursor of braid, are more difficult to attach neatly, and a simple loop sewn in the end of the fly line and looped to the leader is often the best method (*see* diagram).

Tapered nylon leaders can be glued inside the fly line. A hole is made by inserting a large needle 1in (2cm) or more up the core of the line then heating it to burn and seal a hole. The leader is cut to a point and slightly roughened. Cynoacrilate glue is then applied to the butt, and the leader slid up and glued inside the line. The result is a smooth join and the method can also be used to join the backing, especially shooting-head backing, to the line.

Cast connectors are tubes of smooth, strong nylon. By threading leader and line in alternate ends and knotting, they hold the two together in a sure, if rather lumpy embrace, but they do not float too well. Being the traditionalists they are, fly fishermen sometimes opt for one of two methods when joining fly line to leader

which need attention away from the water. One is the needle knot, the other is the neatly sewn and whipped loop (*see* diagram). Strip the coating from 2in (5cm) of the tip of the fly line, fold it back on itself, sew it together, and whip over the join with fly-tying silk, then coat and soak the whole thing in cynoacrilate glue. Such loops at the end of the fly line are particularly useful with sunk-line tactics where leader length can be very important. They are also useful for novice casters who may opt for a length of level nylon leader and finally, the loops allow a quick change of leader, when wind and casting errors tangle it.

Many British anglers favour a permanently needle-knotted butt piece with a loop on the end, to which they then attach their required leader nylon. As has been suggested, tapered leaders are of most use on rivers, and less so with the long-leader tactics that score on stillwater, which possibly reflects the British preference for the more easily available reservoir sport. With the leader attached, the angler may want to add further lengths of nylon, either in the shape of a fine tippet, or a leader with one or more droppers, such as those necessary for the classic loch-style or various nymphing techniques.

The author has total confidence in the water knot for these droppers, and while the well-read novice will read of others he need look no further. The water knot, also known in the UK as the Cove knot, is simply tied and will produce reliable droppers (*see* diagram). If it does not, the nylon, the knot tying, or knot testing tech-

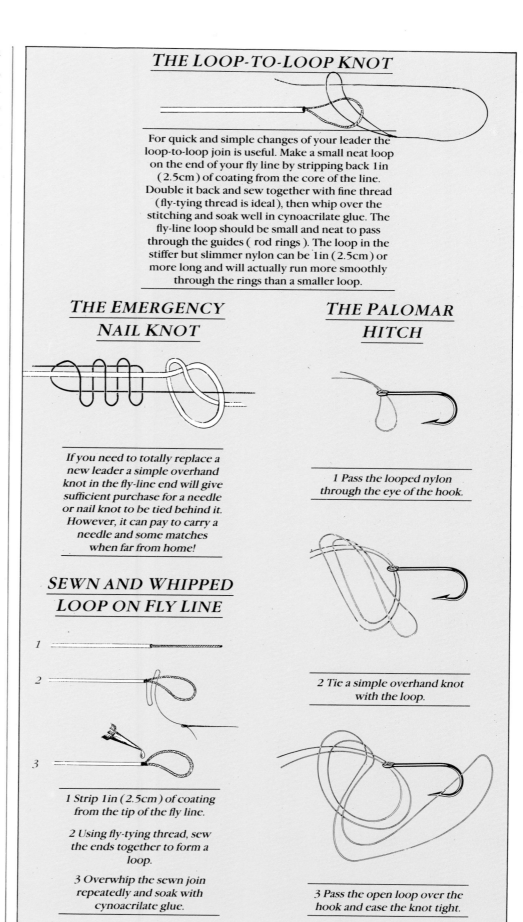

THE LOOP-TO-LOOP KNOT

For quick and simple changes of your leader the loop-to-loop join is useful. Make a small neat loop on the end of your fly line by stripping back 1in (2.5cm) of coating from the core of the line. Double it back and sew together with fine thread (fly-tying thread is ideal), then whip over the stitching and soak well in cynoacrilate glue. The fly-line loop should be small and neat to pass through the guides (rod rings). The loop in the stiffer but slimmer nylon can be 1in (2.5cm) or more long and will actually run more smoothly through the rings than a smaller loop.

THE EMERGENCY NAIL KNOT

If you need to totally replace a new leader a simple overhand knot in the fly-line end will give sufficient purchase for a needle or nail knot to be tied behind it. However, it can pay to carry a needle and some matches when far from home!

SEWN AND WHIPPED LOOP ON FLY LINE

1

2

3

1 Strip 1in (2.5cm) of coating from the tip of the fly line.

2 Using fly-tying thread, sew the ends together to form a loop.

3 Overwhip the sewn join repeatedly and soak with cynoacrilate glue.

THE PALOMAR HITCH

1 Pass the looped nylon through the eye of the hook.

2 Tie a simple overhand knot with the loop.

3 Pass the open loop over the hook and ease the knot tight.

nique are at fault.

So, with line and leader indivisibly knotted, and the reel placed on the rod with the handle to the side of the angler's preference, wind the line on so that it comes through the line guard with which most reels are fitted, at the bottom of the standard fly reel. Thread the line through the rings but not, of course, through the very small keeper ring, sometimes set at right angles to the other rings and always very close to the handle. This ring is generally far too small to be a rod ring, and when present is designed to hold the fly when the angler is on the move.

To attach the fly or flies, you have two useful choices, the blood knot for small flies, always tucked as shown, or the Palomar hitch for larger patterns, mainly lures or salmon flies (*see* diagrams). Both knots are simple to tie, and should be lubricated with saliva and gently eased-up tight. Then, like all knots, tested with a steady pressure before a fish gets a chance to ruin the day.

CASTING – SOME FIRST PRINCIPLES

The very best way to learn casting – some would say the only way – is to go to a professional tutor of repute and take a course. Sometimes it is suggested that the prospective fly fisherman should practise over dry land with a piece of wool instead of a fly. It can do no harm, but what is idiotic is to wander down to your local fishery, buy a ticket, then try to learn how to cast. That really is expensive tuition!

I will now describe the main

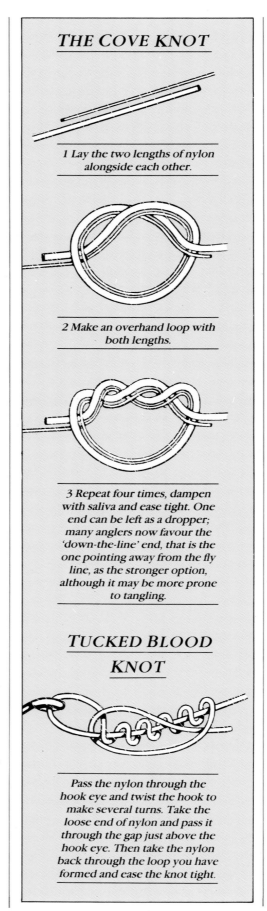

THE COVE KNOT

1 Lay the two lengths of nylon alongside each other.

2 Make an overhand loop with both lengths.

3 Repeat four times, dampen with saliva and ease tight. One end can be left as a dropper; many anglers now favour the 'down-the-line' end, that is the one pointing away from the fly line, as the stronger option, although it may be more prone to tangling.

TUCKED BLOOD KNOT

Pass the nylon through the hook eye and twist the hook to make several turns. Take the loose end of nylon and pass it through the gap just above the hook eye. Then take the nylon back through the loop you have formed and ease the knot tight.

casts and the order in which you should attempt to master them.

ROLL CAST Many leading casting instructors start their pupils off with this cast – and it makes sense. The roll cast is used where there is little space for a back cast, due to trees or high banks. The basic action is to pull enough line from the top ring to load the rod and to lay the line on the water by dropping it at your feet. Then lift the rod firmly and push it back, attempting to drive the rod top into the water. The action is staggering for the novice, but it lifts the line off the surface and drives it out over the water. It is a cast important in most casting manoeuvres, being essential to facilitate lifting off line before the actual cast. In some techniques, notably the stillwater lure and the classic loch-style, it is virtually impossible to fish properly without the ability to perform an extremely competent roll cast – and it is an easy cast.

OVERHEAD CAST This is the basic cast which most fly fishermen use almost all of the time. Master this cast and the rest will, or should, come easily. Follow it through the basic movements: after rolling the line off and laying it out fairly straight in front of you, raise the rod sharply to just beyond the 90 degree mark. Pause fractionally, and the line should fly out behind you. After the line has straightened behind you drive the rod forward and it should shoot out in front of you. Stop the rod at 45 degrees and the line should turn over and roll out straight in front of you. Repeat the process. The timing is all-important; insufficient line speed, or too short or too long a pause at the top of the cast, will

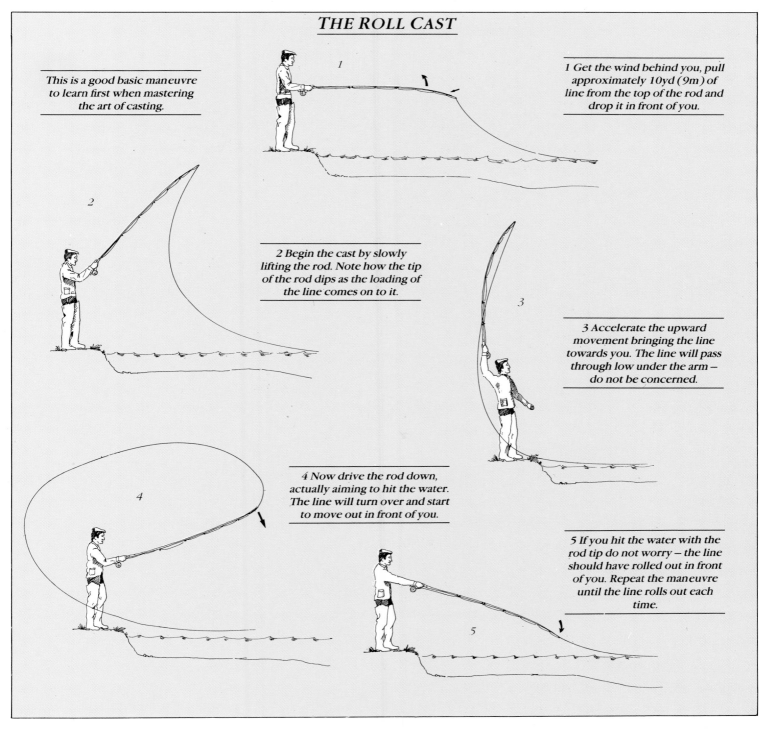

THE ROLL CAST

This is a good basic maneuvre to learn first when mastering the art of casting.

1 *Get the wind behind you, pull approximately 10yd (9m) of line from the top of the rod and drop it in front of you.*

2 *Begin the cast by slowly lifting the rod. Note how the tip of the rod dips as the loading of the line comes on to it.*

3 *Accelerate the upward movement bringing the line towards you. The line will pass through low under the arm — do not be concerned.*

4 *Now drive the rod down, actually aiming to hit the water. The line will turn over and start to move out in front of you.*

5 *If you hit the water with the rod tip do not worry — the line should have rolled out in front of you. Repeat the maneuvre until the line rolls out each time.*

result in hopeless casts, or tangles of the worst kind.

SINGLE-HAUL CASTING If you can hold the 30ft (9m) of line (which balances your rod) in the air consistently (aerialize it), the next move is to improve your casting distance. Striving for distance — *not* accuracy — is the eternal curse of

the stillwater angler who is fishing blind over large expanses of water. But long-casting skills are often necessary, and to cast further the novice will discover he must increase line speed. Hauls on the line as he casts are the way to achieve line speed. Hauls are not violent tugs, they must be pro-

perly orchestrated so that they fit into the cast in one smooth, fluid coordination of hand, arm and eye.

Start by holding the fly line in the left hand as you cast with the right. This automatically gives you the beginnings of a single haul. Now extend this grip on the line into a smooth downward haul (in

THE OVERHEAD CAST

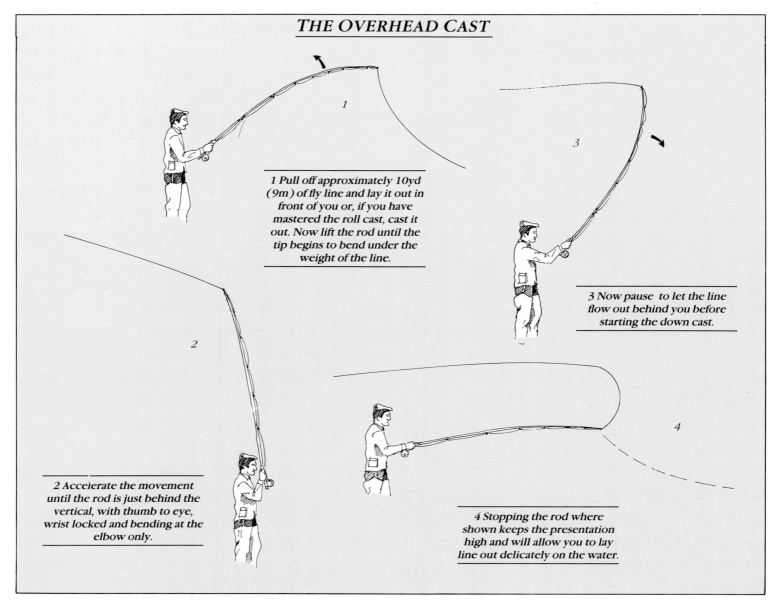

1 Pull off approximately 10yd (9m) of fly line and lay it out in front of you or, if you have mastered the roll cast, cast it out. Now lift the rod until the tip begins to bend under the weight of the line.

3 Now pause to let the line flow out behind you before starting the down cast.

2 Accelerate the movement until the rod is just behind the vertical, with thumb to eye, wrist locked and bending at the elbow only.

4 Stopping the rod where shown keeps the presentation high and will allow you to lay line out delicately on the water.

the same vertical line as your rod) as you lift the flyline from the water, so accelerating the speed of the line through the air.

Now use the same smooth haul after the line has straightened out behind you – this also accelerates the line and, coupled with the correct moment of release, pushes your cast out further. A weight-forward or shooting-head line is necessary to use this cast to full effect.

DOUBLE-HAUL CASTING This is the standard cast for the angler who needs to reach for distance. To

double haul, you perform both the motions described above – that is you accelerate the line as you lift off, then haul after it straightens out behind you to speed it forward. As in all casting, timing is more important than brute strength, and all the movements will look effortless as you watch a professional cast out a full weight-forward line.

SIDE CAST To keep the line under obstructions on the back cast, or to put the fly under an obstruction on the front cast, you need to master the side cast. To achieve this you simply turn all the basic

overhead casting actions on their side, with the rod horizontal or at least at an angle to the vertical. As the line will be closer to the ground or water, a good hauling technique is vital to keep the line moving fast, and to produce a tight loop.

THE LOOP AND CASTING Every cast produces a loop in the line, behind or above the angler. This is caused when the fly line gradually unfolds behind the angler. The faster the line movement, the tighter the loop and the tighter the loop, the greater the risk of a tangle. So when double-hauling for distance

THE SIDE CAST

on a big stillwater, with a single nymph or lure, you might manage it without tangles. You will, however, need a leader that is not too long, and you may have to avoid the dragging effect of a heavily weighted fly. When casting a team of flies, perhaps a traditional wet fly cast or a team of chironomid imitations, to haul too quickly is to invite tangles and you need to cultivate a wide, slow loop and accept some loss of casting distance.

STEEPLE CAST You can also make that tight loop form a steeple above you. This is a useful cast when there are obstructions behind you, and no room to make a proper back-cast. Basically, you change the timing of the cast so that the loop forms horizontally above you, then by the timing of your forward cast, and haul, drive the line out in front. An easier alternative is usually the roll cast, although sometimes the small amount of line that goes behind you on this cast and the low trajectory of the line, make the cast difficult where there is confined space or vegetation under your feet.

DEALING WITH THE WIND Many novice casters consciously seek a bank with a nice, safe left to right wind (or vice-versa for a left-hander), or a back wind that helps to drive out their cast. They may at the same time miss the best of the sport, so it pays to have one or two tricks to overcome the wind. The way to cast into the wind is to achieve a low delivery. If you imagine that there is a 2-ft (0.6-m) gap below the wind, and aim your cast and delivery below that height, you will cast considerably farther than if you chose to fight the wind. When threatened with a vicious side wind which tends to blow each cast into the side of your head, the easiest way to overcome the problem is simply to turn your back on the water, and make your 'back cast' in front of you, then shoot the line back over your shoulder. This also gives you a good view of your back cast (which is now the 'actual' cast) and enables you to improve its direction and timing.

SAFETY No mention of fly casting and the problem of wind would be complete without a brief reminder

Side casting under an obstruction calls for the same speed, accuracy and timing as for the overhead cast, but the moves are performed on the horizontal.

to always wear a hat (and possibly a turned-up collar or scarf) and sunglasses, both when fishing and practising casting. As has already been stated in the tackle section, both a hat and glasses have a role to play in helping you catch more fish as well as protecting your face and head.

Even practising with a tuft of wool in place of a fly is no defence. A high-speed fly line slapping your face is an excruciating and potentially damaging thing. Bearing that in mind, always consider bystanders and spectators when practising and watch where your back cast is going. Even the most expert fly casters forget to check this, and their victims are mainly trees. Yours might be something less resilient.

In the world of casting, first good tuition, then practice, makes perfect as nothing else will.

THE FLY FISHERMAN'S FISH

ALMOST every fish that swims will take a fly from time to time. And, of course, a fly can be tied to imitate a huge range of food items that will tempt them. But the fish listed in this chapter are the main quarry of the fly fisherman – plus a few personal choices, included for reasons that hopefully will become clear to the reader.

TROUT

BROWN TROUT (*Salmo trutta*)

To some extent the hero of our book, the brown trout is either indigenous, or stocked, all over the world. Brown is an odd description of a fish that can be as black as coal, or as silver as any salmon, depending on the season and its location. For instance the brown trout of Lough Carra in Ireland are silver blue, but about 100 miles (161km) away, on Lough Melvin, they are virtually black. *Salmo trutta* is a hardy species, surviving in some comparatively unlikely settings, needing only clean, well-oxygenated flowing water with gravel beds to spawn successfully. It will also migrate to the sea, staying close to the coast, and return up rivers and into sea lochs when it will generally be known as the sea trout.

RAINBOW TROUT (*Salmo gairdneri*)

This is another trout that has responded well to stocking all over the world, having been introduced from the US. In a few places, in the UK and other countries, it has successfully established breeding populations. Mostly, however, away from the US, the species has relied on the fish farmer and stocking programmes for its presence. 'Rainbow' refers to the fish's bright coloration, mainly a reddish-purple banding along its side. With constant stocking in Europe, its sea-run form, the steelhead, is beginning to turn up in rivers and sea lochs in northern Europe, including the Baltic Sea, but the numbers are minute compared to the vast runs that make the steelhead a prized target on the Pacific seaboard of the US and Canada.

CUT-THROAT TROUT (*Salmo clarki*)

Named for the vivid slash of colour at its throat, the cut-throat is common in the western US up to Alaska. This fish, too, will wander out to sea at the mouths of rivers, acquiring the bright silver of the sea trout or steelhead.

These beautiful stillwater rainbows have fine tails and fins.

TOP LEFT *An immaculate wild brown trout from Colorado's Eagle River. Compare with a wild brown from the Frying Pan River, Colorado (*MIDDLE LEFT*).*

BOTTOM LEFT *A fine steelhead is displayed.*

ABOVE *A 3-lb (1.4-kg) rainbow ready for return to the Frying Pan River.*

OPPOSITE TOP *This specimen Wyoming cut-throat trout ended up as a trophy.*

OPPOSITE MIDDLE *This American brook trout was taken from a deep lake in the Rocky Mountains of Colorado.*

OPPOSITE BOTTOM *The king of game fish – a 27-lb (12-kg) Atlantic salmon from Norway's River Vosso.*

BROOK TROUT (*Salvelinus fontinalis*)
Known in Europe as the American brook trout, or charr (which it strictly speaking is) this is the most beautiful of the common trout in its cream and tomato-soup colours. A denizen of the eastern half of the US, the fish is being hounded out of its traditional homes by imported browns and rainbows. This species will not only do well in brooks but also exists comfortably in stillwater. Given the chance, it will also go to sea – but with the pollution of the East Coast such sea-run fish are rare these days.

THE DOLLY VARDEN (*Salvelinus malmo*)
A handsome near-relative of the brook trout, the Dolly Varden is a West Coast trout, often encountered in Alaska. Yet another occasional traveller to sea.

SALMON

THE ATLANTIC SALMON (*Salmo salar*)
Salar, the leaper, known as the king of fish, runs from the northern Atlantic into rivers in the US and Europe and also from the North Sea into the UK, Norway and the Baltic Sea. Stocks of Atlantic salmon are now severely threatened by netting in the ocean, and by acid rain and the damming of its home rivers. The salmon is a prime fighter, given to leaps and long runs. It does not feed in freshwater and must be tempted to take a fly.

PACIFIC SALMON

CHINOOK (*Oncorhynchus tschawytscha*) The chinook is also known as king or spring salmon, names that betray the respect in which it is held, and the time of its first runs.

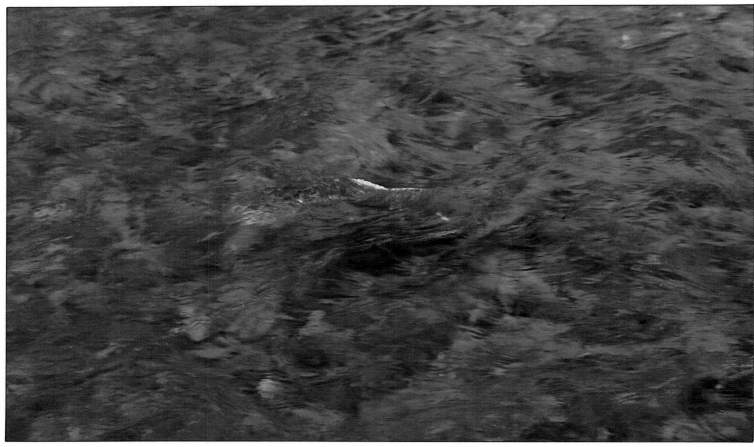

SILVER or **COHO** (*Oncorhynchus kisutch*) This salmon does not match the size of the chinook, and makes a solid three-month run during the year. It can also be taken in the sea.

BLUEBACK (or **SOCKEYE**) (*Oncorhynchus nerka*); **DOG** (or **CHUM**) (*Oncorhynchus keta*); **HUMPBACK** (or **PINK**) (*Oncorhynchus gorbuscha*) Three other species of salmon that run in vast numbers, and provide the bulk of sport on the western seaboard of the US.

OTHER FRESHWATER FISH

GRAYLING (*Thymallus thymallus*); **ARCTIC GRAYLING** (*Thymallus arcticus*) The grayling is a scaled fish,

OPPOSITE ABOVE A specimen king salmon from Lake Michigan.

OPPOSITE BELOW A sockeye salmon on its spawning run.

ABOVE A coho salmon from Lake Michigan.

common throughout the Northern hemisphere in one or other of the two species, but particularly so in Alaska and in Lapland. Despite its overslung mouth, typical of a bottom feeder, the grayling will rise well to a fly.

MUSKELLUNGE (*Esox masquinongy*); **NORTHERN PIKE** (*Esox lucius*) Both powerful predators, very similar in appearance, the muskellunge is found only in the US and Canada, while the smaller but equally aggressive northern pike extends throughout North America, Europe and Asia. Both fish are excellent hunters with superb dentation, they can be taken on bucktail streamers, though the fly angler would be advised to employ a wire trace on his leader.

PERCH (*Perca fluviatilis*); **YELLOW PERCH** (*Perca flavescens*) The European perch and its American relative are so similar that they can be treated as one fish for angling purposes. Handsome with their stripes and spined dorsal fin, they are easy to catch on a light fly rod, pulled adequately when hooked, and are included because this author thinks they eat better than any other freshwater fish – salmon included!

LARGEMOUTH BASS (*Micropterus*) **SMALLMOUTH BASS** (*dolomieu*) Both of these handsome spiky-backed American gamefish will take a

ABOVE LEFT Grayling from a stream in Derbyshire, England. Though these fell to bait, they readily take a fly.

ABOVE RIGHT A northern pike of 28lb (13kg) from an English stillwater.

RIGHT A yellow perch hooked on bait – they take flies too and eat superbly well.

streamer lure; and the largemouth will rise particularly well to surface flies, making for some of the most exciting fly fishing going.

BLUEGILL (*Lepomis macrochirus*) Of all the American panfish that will take a fly, the bluegill sunfish is included because it is the perfect fish for a beginner, and this writer will never forget a quiet sun-drenched afternoon in Georgia, US, flipping a popping bug in under the trees on a fly rod, and hooking fish after fish. The bug even outfished worms that day, sometimes drawing up bluegills the size of postage stamps.

SEA FISH

TARPON (*Tarpon atlanticus*) Most sea fish will take a fly, but this huge silver beast must be the ultimate challenge, growing to hundreds of pounds or kilograms and fighting with leaps and runs that few fish can match.

BONEFISH (*Albula vulpes*) This is the great visual sea fish for the fly fisher. Moving in groups over shallow, often wadable water the bonefish must be cast to and when hooked they set off at high speed, often running long distances.

LEFT *Two good largemouth bass from a Missouri lake.*

ABOVE *Back goes a fine bonefish.*

RIGHT *A specimen smallmouth bass from Lake Michigan.*

THE WATERS WE FISH

*F*LY fishermen owe a great deal to a handsome spotted creature known as the brown trout. Its range through the Northern hemisphere and its importation below the equator, meant that the most interesting and challenging fish the fly fisherman seeks is widely available. Not the least reason for this is the trout's remarkable ability to feed, breed and reproduce in almost any clean stillwater with some sort of feeder stream, or in a wide range of rivers and streams from the smallest to the largest.

Most of the other game fish will be found in similar locations. The various migratory species, the salmon, steelhead and sea trout require access to the sea – but river-fed lakes and lochs will have their runs. If the waters worth the fly fisherman's attention are varied, so are the locations where his quarry may be found. Only local knowledge will answer some of the questions posed at various locations, but several things are certain. Fish will be found where they may stay in safety, where there is an adequate supply of food and where they may expend the minimum energy. There are exceptions to these general rules, and

they will mainly exist when fish find their actions governed by spawning urges.

Where 'aggression' replaces a natural feeding urge, behaviour patterns can change and this is the greatest fascination in pursuing the Atlantic salmon. But bearing in mind the basic rules, consider the fly fisherman's many venues, and where his fly may most effectively be cast.

SMALL STREAMS

These may be alkaline and rich in food or sparse and acid. Generally the anglers' target will be brown trout, brook trout, rainbows and grayling, and in various venues they will range up to several pounds or kilos. Such fish will always be challenging, and the best fish will hold in the most protected lies, where food comes easily. To do this, fish will see off all smaller interlopers, even eating them. In the sparser streams, generally in hill or mountain country, there will be very few specimen trout compared with hundreds of smaller ones. They get larger by finding the best lies, and they should be sought in the deeper

Fishing below a waterfall on the River Lyon in Scotland for Atlantic salmon.

holes, below undercut banks, wherever fallen trees or boulders create snags, and wherever a quirk of the current collects food in a steady stream.

The experienced angler will consider such areas, discovering which method will best present his fly to the fish. It might be a large dry fly, plopped heavily over the lie, a heavily loaded nymph dunked into the fish's lair, or a lure or small fish imitation swum enticingly by. Long casts or heavy tackle are rarely necessary on the jump-across streams. What is necessary is the belly-to-the-ground commando-style approach; and an almost second-sighted ability to sniff out the lie of

LEFT Tiny streams almost always yield small fish – but even so, they offer incredibly challenging fishing.

ABOVE Delightful and enchanting surroundings add an air of mystery to this creek in North Carolina.

a better fish. No prizes are given for standing on the skyline or thrashing the water to foam with a bad cast. Mastery of the underwater currents is useful too; once it is in the water, getting the fly down, across, or under to a trout can be very difficult. This is no place for petty restrictions of up-stream or downstream – the fly

must be flicked, catapulted, or twitched into place.

MEDIUM-SIZED RIVERS

Here our quarry may be any one of the game fish, and the nature of the stream can be infinitely variable – from the lush green of the Test or Itchen in Hampshire's green chalk-stream meadow land, to the rugged rocks of the Snake or Rogue rivers in the western US; from the acid upland salmon rivers such as the Airey of south-west Scotland, racing to the sea in a few miles of spate river, to the steady trundle of dredged and canalized middle sections of rivers everywhere, featureless and dull but often full of

trout. Somewhere in this group you can place most of the classic trout streams of the world and quite a few of the best rivers for migratory species. With the salmon, sea trout and steelhead there are infinite possibilities, and only local knowledge will clearly mark all the lies and runs that the fish will occupy. But a trout is a trout, and it will pay to consider a number of natural features that will always attract the fish.

Under some conditions – low water, extreme warmth, slight pollution deoxygenating the water, extremely clear water – you may find trout in the fast streamy runs provided there is sufficient depth. Certainly you will find small trout,

ABOVE Streamy water of this sort fishes best for trout in times of drought – otherwise small fish may be your reward.

OPPOSITE LEFT A powerfully flowing but deep river offers many problems for the fly fisherman.

OPPOSITE RIGHT Idaho's Salmon River boasts an excellent run of steelhead.

grayling, and salmon parr in the streamy sections and they will be easily caught. For the better trout, however, look for areas where the current divides, around a rock, or other obstruction, or splits, leaving slack areas, eddies, undercuts or deep boiling pot-holes. Fish these areas with care, avoiding extremely deep slow water, or canal-like sections which often seem devoid of trout.

Manmade features are to be found on many of these waters; bridges shelter fish – often the uncatchable giants – and change the flow where their standings push aside the current. Likewise groynes pushing out into the flow, weirs and other obstructions such as

TROUT LIES ON THE RIVER

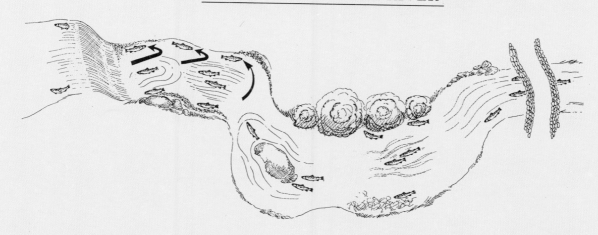

Starting at the left with the weir or waterfall, note the two lies at each corner – smart trout appreciate how difficult it is to put an artificial fly over them here. Below the falls, note that in the eddies trout may be facing the 'wrong' way. These fish may also be under the bank in undercuts. On the nearside, two trout lie among the swirling fronds of weed – an awkward position to get a nymph to. In the middle in the fast shallows will be mainly small fish – except, that is, in times of drought when all the fish will appreciate the extra oxygenation of this area. Note the fish around the boulders. Trout will frequently lie in the shelter behind boulders – perversely trout and migratory fish sometimes tuck in where the current splits in front of the boulders.

Under the trees on the north bank is an obvious lie. The lower and more awkward the trees the better – it is safer for the fish and a regular food supply falls from above. More fish lie in the shelter of the weeds on the south bank. There is food here too, and even right in the middle of the open water the fish feel secure. In the undercut of the bend, under some dead roots, lies a specimen trout who will only come out for a big fish-like lure. Trout adore the shelter of the bridge, but in front of them one good trout lies in apparently open water. He has found that the current sweeping back across the bend brings a constant supply of food.

waterfalls, cut their own deep
pools and radically change the
speed and nature of a river. Man
may also be responsible for the
bankside trees and bushes which
can overhang the water, collecting
weed and food and sheltering
trout. Inch worms, beetles and
other insects fall from this vegetation to feed the sheltering fish.

Where the undermining force
of the river becomes too much, a
tree may topple into the river,
again attracting and sheltering fish,
and providing a nightmare of snags
for the unwary angler. Rocks in the
river also affect the flow and shelter fish, sometimes in the deflec-
tion of water upstream but more
often below. A wide range of casts
will be needed to reach these fish,
to cover the water, and most im-
portantly to fish the fly properly.

LARGE RIVERS

Chasing the salmon and other
migratory fish of these waters has
its own problems, and the long
European fly rods of up to 18ft
(5.5m) or more, with heavy double-
taper lines, were often seen as the
solution. Now even on the most
traditional of Scottish rivers there

ABOVE *Some stretches of Scotland's mighty River Spey need long-casting to cover the salmon lies.*

LEFT *The Yellowstone River.*

OPPOSITE TOP *Fishing a mighty Alaskan river.*

OPPOSITE MIDDLE *Many of Norway's best rivers have been devastated by acid rain.*

OPPOSITE BOTTOM *Some Norwegian rivers widen into huge lakes.*

is the beginning of a change, already taken place elsewhere, to an outfit such as the standard heavy fly-fishing outfit described in Chapter 1, with shooting heads and plenty of backing. But wading the classic large rivers such as the Tweed or Spey with chest waders and a long fly rod is an art of itself.

All that is true of the other bodies of running water is true of the large rivers. Mentally break them down into smaller streams, put on the waders, and get out to positions that allow you to properly fish your fly through what looks like a recognizable lie – it may be a huge boulder sheltering a salmon, a situation which, in miniature, you have observed before on a tiny mountain trout stream.

STILLWATERS

Waters of this kind do not always run deep, and trout may be taken in shallow pools, stocked or unstocked, less than 10ft (3m) deep – shallower still if the owner or manager is around to protect his stock and keep the predators away. Shallow, clear pools of under 10 acres (4 hectares) are best treated like a river. Trout in a stillwater environment are more inclined to cruise about than the river-borne fish. A wide, steady river pool may hold cruising, feeding trout moving on top; a stillwater will invariably have some cruising fish, especially if rainbows are among the stock.

I remember one pool where all the rainbows cruised in open, if weeded, water, while the browns stayed close under marginal trees, rising to terrestrial insects falling

WHERE TO FISH ON STILLWATER

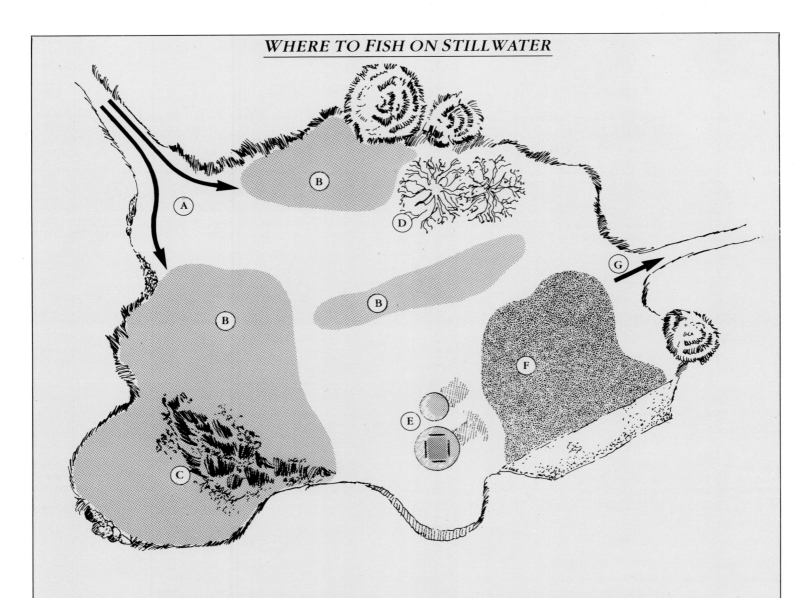

This imaginary map gives you the clues:

A The entry of a river or stream. Late or early in the season, this will hold post- or pre-spawning trout. In warm periods the water will be more oxygenated here and trout may gather to take advantage. When the stream is in flood it will bring both food and possibly quantities of silt into the lake. Trout are very partial to earthworms, but less keen on being blinded by muddy water.

B These areas are shallows. You may well take fish from the bank over these areas early and late in the day – fish will move onto the shallows to feed at night. However, the central shallow area may well be a boat fishing hotspot, especially when worked over-the-front, loch style.

C This is an area of weedbeds. This will be particularly attractive to the fish that move in to feed at dusk, and will probably hold some trout all day. It will be good too in the early season when last year's dead weeds will hold what remains of the food supply.

D These dead trees or sticks in the water will be a hotspot at fry-feeding time. Here the little prey fish will try to shelter (as they will in the weedbeds) and the trout will seek them out. The sticks may also shelter newly stocked trout.

E This area will also shelter prey fish, and being over deeper water will attract some of the better fish. This is a tower or other structure and there may well be underwater pipes or aerators near it, all of which attract fish.

F This is an area of deeper water. Here big lures and fast-sinking lines may take some better fish. This area has been artificially deepened by the building of a dam. The corners of the dam will always hold fish, particularly stocked trout, and fishing anywhere along the dam wall with a fast-sinker and a bouyant fly may produce specimen trout.

G This is the river's exit. If this is a loch or lough with access to the sea, this may be the hotspot to intercept migratory trout and salmon.

in. I took a limit of fish nymphing with a Woolly Worm pattern. Dried out and cast as a dry fly, it took a fine brown that had risen persistently under a bankside tree. Much of the sport with these cruising fish is visual. They must be picked off as they cruise past, and often you get but one chance. Presentation and cast must be perfect, right down to the sinking speed of your fly.

Otherwise, on the small clear waters look for features similar to those found in rivers that hold trout — especially any weedbeds. Small, coloured stillwaters are better prospected with a bright lure or wet fly initially. Eventually they may offer superb sport to nymph or even dry fly, but trout in coloured water provide an unnatural situation, one in which they may become just bottom grubbers.

RESERVOIRS — THE EUROPEAN STANDBY

The thriving British stillwater trouting scene — indeed the whole British trouting scene — relies greatly on a series of heavily stocked water-supply reservoirs. One at least, Rutland Water, approaches the delights and problems of a wild fishery in its size and complexity. Here, trout get time to grow on and become somewhat feral. Other, more circular waters give their fish less chance of escape, and consequently have a high turnover of stock. Stock-pen fed

trout can be easy targets because these fish know man as the provider of food, not as a predator. Few of these waters manage any degree of recruitment among their trout stocks. Some browns breed in their feeder streams, and the occasional rainbow parr appears on some waters, but angling pressure and the natural order demands heavy stocking. Similar waters are to be found world-wide, and there is a rapidly growing interest in this style of sport in France. But it is mainly in the UK where the vast majority of these waters remain fly only.

Reservoir trouting has led to the invention of a number of borderline fly-fishing techniques in many ways more akin to trolling

ABOVE Worldwide contrasts: master British nymph angler Gordon Fraser plays a rainbow on a small put-and-take water in Northamptonshire, England (left); but Ringstead Grange's few acres would be swallowed thousands of times in this Arkansas reservoir, home of many game fish species (right).

and spinning, but worthy of interest for the success they have enjoyed with deep-lying trout over the past two decades. Otherwise this fishing is full of variety, with a huge range of tactics producing trout of varying degrees of quality. In the rich English Midland reservoirs — Grafham, Eye Brook, Rutland — trout will feed naturally a week or so after stocking, and

sometimes treble their weight in a season, particularly the fast growing rainbows. With a hundred years of high-quality sport behind it, the British stillwater scene must be taken seriously. The worldwide fly fishing scene already owes it a debt for evolving new styles, methods and flies.

LARGER NATURAL LAKES, LOCHS AND LOUGHS

All over the world there are naturally stocked, high-quality trout lakes, each with their own strains of trout. Some of them support mixed populations of game fish, especially where there is access to a major river or better still the sea.

Consider Lough Melvin on the borders of Eire and Ulster. Here there are four genetically different strains of *Salmo trutta* – browns, ferox and the delightfully named sonneghan and gillaroo, salmon and, in the depths, charr. Though the lough is acid, and low on food, for some reason there are no sea trout – the browns never migrate to sea.

Fishing such waters is a delight, the classic British loch-style, as it is known, is as likely to draw up and hook a 9-oz (255-gm) brown as a 9-lb (4-kg) salmon – I know, I've done both on one day. The historical richness of the great Irish loughs – Corrib, Conn, Mask, and the great Scottish lochs – Leven, Watten, or Orkney's Harray, has a charm irrelevant to fishing, which enhances it even more. Here, some of the great international fly patterns saw their birth, flies which though tied for one species do great slaughter of another 3,000 miles (4,800km) away. Old boats and old boatmen still ply these waters, and though the modern skills and styles of fly fishing may eventually revolutionize the sport on such waters, change will be long and slow.

BELOW Britain's largest reservoir, Rutland Water, offers splendid boat fishing in its two arms – especially for the loch-style angler.

STILLWATER FISHING: FINDING THE FISH

'Stillwater' is a misnomer. It is in fact never still, whether the movement comes from pressure and temperature change, wind, or the action of feeder streams. Underwater currents are as significant to trout as more visible river currents are. They will push food around, and trout are lazy enough to wait for its arrival at their noses. Cruising fish will generally move upwind, even at depth. More static populations of trout can be sought around structures, natural or manmade. Dam walls seem to have a universal appeal to all trout in most conditions and seasons.

ABOVE *The expert Lough Melvin boatman, Vinnie Battisti, tries a cast or two as his clients take a break – his spare hand steers the boat with a trailing oar.*

RIGHT *A sea trout forges its way up the Yorkshire Esk.*

Towers, piers and other structures that shelter small fish will bring the predatory trout in. Feeder streams will often attract trout late and early in their season, usually drawn by spawning urges, sometimes to feed on the roe and young of other spawners.

Weedbeds are worthy of attention, and even on the largest stillwater, odd natural features sometime cause fish to tarry. A salmon moving into a sea loch on its way to the spawning grounds may pause by the end of a stone wall or fence – there is no apparent logic but it happens too often to be coincidence.

Generally, on the very large waters, a ghillie, boatman, or guide is a safe investment. Even on the homely lowland waters of England, some employ boatmen; on the vastness of a Scottish loch, Irish lough or the huge North American lakes, there is also the safety factor to consider. Much of the best trout fishing water on any huge lake is shallow. On some, huge fish may be taken in quite shallow water. On many waters, sharp sub-surface rocks are always a threat in the best fishing areas.

Fly fishing tactics are not really applicable to the very big deep-water lake trout, or the British ferox. There are deep fishing methods, but they lack finesse. Never neglect shallow water surrounded by deeps (what the Irish logically call a sunken island), for it will hold your best stillwater chance of finding big fish that will take your fly.

You will find more about fish location in Chapter 6. To sum up, think trout on all waters. Think lazy fish which prefer the current to bring the food. Think safety, shelter, and a pecking order that means the best spots, often the most difficult to fish, invariably hold the best fish. And having considered all that, your fish of a lifetime from a stillwater will probably come from nowhere in a blur over an unconsidered spot. May that fish not depart as quickly when your time comes.

FLIES AND FLY LIFE

*T*HE fish that the fly fisherman pursues have one thing in common. They will eat food items that the fly dresser can imitate by tying materials onto a hook that the fly rod and line can cast. In the vast majority of cases, the 'fly' will mean an imitation of a preyfish; when pursuing trout and grayling it will most often be an insect or crustacean that is imitated; and when after migratory fish that do not feed in freshwater it may be simply a fancy fly that lures the fish into biting rather than attempting to feed.

PREY FISH AND THEIR IMITATION

First we will consider the small prey fish that the vast majority of fly-rod caught species feed on. It is not possible to attempt to list them here, but certain rules can be applied to the imitation of such creatures. Generally they will be 3–4in (8–10cm) long at the most – anything larger is very difficult to cast. The bodies of the living creatures may be a wide range of colours, and they may swim in various ways. Eels and lampreys will have a sinuous movement;

small bottom-living fish will dart with a stop-start movement; mid-water fish seem to move with a steady flutter; a wounded fish will often have depth-control difficulties, tending to struggle up and down as it moves along. Most of these prey fish have large obvious eyes, and imitations will incorporate bead chain or plastic artificial eyes; while jungle cock substitute, or painted-on eyes are highly effective.

Other materials can be used for scaled or irridescent bodies, mylar tubing, or one of the newer pearlescent-type tubes, or slips of flat prismatic tape are all excellent. Plain flat tinsel, and chenille are also effective. To imitate the swimming movements of the fish, wings incorporating bucktail, squirrel, maribou, and the newer flexible metallic and pearlescent materials are often employed.

Another winging system incorporates strips of rabbit or other fur tied along the back of the fly. To mimic the often prominent heads of small fish, deer hair muddler-style, or bullet-style, and gill-shaped spade feathers can be effective. For imitations of smaller fish in their transluscent fry stage,

A colourful selection of salmon flies.

bodies are wound of clear stretched polythene over a sparse silver wrap on the hook shank.

Despite all these opportunities for close-copy patterns of fry, and the known success of flies such as the Muddler Minnow, contrary creatures like trout may fall to simple patterns like the Mission-ary, or the Baby Doll – simply a white fish-shaped wrap of wool – and even to all black flies.

Imitation points for prey fish and fry: pronounced eye; slim bodies, possibly with pronounced head; wings with plenty of action; mixed colour bodies, dark on top, paler underneath.

Small fry are often transluscent. In all cases, body length can be sig-nificant, so hook shanks should re-flect this, or a tandem or other hook mount should be used.

EGGS

Fish on migratory spawning runs, and others just taking advantage of available feed, often take fish eggs. These are generally imitated best by egg-shaped balls of transluscent dubbing, chenille, or wool, spun muddler-deer-hair fashion.

TOP LEFT *A good imitator of a typical prey fish – a bottom skulking bullhead, tied muddler-style.*

MIDDLE LEFT *Nothing could be simpler than Frank Sawyer's Killer Bug – but fish taking shrimps devour it with gusto.*

LEFT *The Red Spot Shrimp is an effective scud or freshwater shrimp pattern.*

OPPOSITE TOP *A freshwater crayfish – big fish of many species enjoy this delicacy.*

OPPOSITE BELOW *A pattern from Australia which imitates the yabby or freshwater crayfish.*

CRUSTACEA

Prawn, shrimp, and in the ocean, crab patterns have been tied and successfully used. Prawn imitations are particularly effective for Atlantic salmon, while shrimp patterns are used in the pursuit of bonefish and other salt water species. The trout, too, greedily accepts a meal of scuds, sowbugs, and occasionally crayfish. All imitations will have a shellback, made of feather fibre, raffia, plastic, and so on, pulled over a body of softer material, usually a dubbing mix, with legs imitated by guard hairs, hackle fibres, bucktail, or on large patterns for Atlantic salmon, golden pheasant feathers.

In freshwater, the colour of the scud or shrimp varies from dark brown through shades of olive green and pale brown to grey. Most imitations will benefit from a shaped hook, to imitate the hunchbacked profile of the shrimp, and in freshwater the pattern should be weighted to swim upside down in the manner of the natural. Superb close-copy crayfish are the preserve of the expert fly dresser, but shrimp imitators are easily tied.

GASTROPODS

It is not often realized that trout feed on freshwater snails. At times they will pick them off the bottom; on other occasions snails indulge

in mass 'migrations' on lakes, float-
ing foot-up in the surface film, and
moving with the current. Many a
mystery rise has been caused by
this warm-weather phenomenon.
The snail is perhaps the only imitation where really bulky patterns
can be effective. For fishing deep a
fat body of peacock herl with a
sparse black hen hackle works
well; at the surface a shaped cork
or piece of balsa wood, or a simple
fly of dark grey dyed deer hair
spun muddler-style will be effective.

INSECTS

And so to the 'real' flies that make
up so much of the diet of trout,
grayling, and the many fly-caught
panfish. Their imitation is the
basis of traditional fly fishing.

MAYFLIES
(EPHEMEROPTERA)

These are also known as dayflies,
and sometimes olives. The
Ephemeroptera, which range from
1½in (3.8cm) giants to barely-
visible Caenis, are of major
interest to the trout and the fly
fisherman. This is the classic fly
that brought the term nymphing

OPPOSITE TOP **Casting to
overhanging trees where
terrestrials will fall onto the water.**

OPPOSITE FAR LEFT **A British pond
olive nymph** – Cloeon dipterum.

OPPOSITE LEFT **A mayfly nymph –
Ephemera danica** – *attempting to burrow.*

TOP RIGHT **A mayfly dun of
Ephemera danica.**

MIDDLE RIGHT **The mayfly adult
or imago of** Ephemera danica.

RIGHT **A blue-winged olive
mayfly or dayfly** Ephemerella
ignita.

FLY FISHING

LEFT Richard Walker's Pheasant Tail Nymph is a deadly artificial.

BELOW LEFT This Sawyer Swedish or Grey Goose Nymph serves well to imitate many of the smaller olives or mayflies.

BOTTOM LEFT Cased caddis larvae clinging to a log.

into fly fishing parlance. Its nymph draws feeding fish up wherever it occurs and in whatever species. It is unmistakable when on the water, its wings upright like a galleon under sail, often equally windswept as it is blown along the surface. And as its ephemeral name suggests, it quickly passes, the adult is short-lived, returning to breed and die within days of hatching.

The eggs laid produce a nymph, which lives and breathes underwater. Eventually the mature nymph moves to the surface, its skin splits, and it climbs onto the floating skin while drying and expanding its wings. Trout feed hungrily on mayflies at this stage. When — and if — the successfully hatched dun or sub imago flies off the water it will rest on the bank for some time, before undergoing another moult of skin, emerging on the bank as a fully fledged imago (known as a spinner by the fly fisherman).

Now in a breeding condition, the mayfly mates, and returns to the water to deposit eggs into the water. Completing this process, the spent insect collapses on the water where the hungry trout are feeding.

Imitation points: nymphs have three tails, and six legs (as do all true insects). The proportion of long, generally slender abdomen to thorax is approximately two-thirds to one-third, and the thorax

is covered by a wing case. Most species also have a fairly distinctive row of gills along the sides of the abdomen. Colours vary from cream to dark chestnut brown, with less of the olive of the adult. Bodies of the artificials will generally be tied of fine dubbing, or feather fibre; wing cases, tails, and legs of feather fibre; emerging patterns can have in-built buoyancy in the shape of greased-up dubbing wing pads.

For adult dry fly patterns similar body and tail materials can be used, though there is a wider range of colours. Wings should be tied upright; or of course to lie flat (or spent) on the water. A huge range of hook sizes exists in both standard and longshank varieties; 22s up to size 8 will be necessary.

THE CADDIS
(*TRICHOPTERA*)

Also known as sedge flies, the Trichoptera resemble moths in their adult form and are grub-like and tubby in their larval and pupal forms. Many caddis flies build cases as larvae to protect themselves against predators. They secrete a 'glue' and use suitable locally available materials to form a protective case around the soft body. Other caddis larvae hide wherever they can. Both kinds are eaten by trout – the caddis, case and all, is eaten

TOP RIGHT An adult caddis or sedge makes a meaty mouthful for a trout.

ABOVE RIGHT Simple cased caddis patterns catch many trout.

RIGHT A useful sedge pupa imitation.

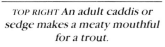

in the early season when other food is scarce. In the next stage, the pupa eventually leaves the case, or hiding place (occasionally just a tube in the river bottom). It is a plump creature that seems a mass of waving legs and feelers with distinctive immature wing buds. Swimming rapidly to the surface, it reaches the top and emerges from the pupal skin with an almost audible plop. Take-off is usually rapid — though some species do struggle across the top of the water as they depart.

Imitation points: Larvae have a distinctive dark head, with a long caterpillar-like body. Unlike the caterpillar, the legs are grouped at the head end. Colours range from a very bright green, through brown, to cream. The cased caddis is easy to imitate, with a long body of suitably rough material, matched to the colour of the naturals, plus a thin band of abdomen colour, topped by a pronounced black head and a sparse hen hackle to imitate legs. The pupa calls for a transluscent dubbed body, plump and wasp-shaped. Wing buds of feather fibre are tied in; and legs are of strands of speckled feather fibres. Adults are distinguished by their roof-shaped wings when at rest.

Again a wide range of hook sizes from 16s to 8s will be suitable.

DRAGONFLIES AND DAMSELFLIES (ODONATA)

Both underwater and above, the Class Odonata comprises deadly predators, feeding on other insects. The adults are unmistakable, flitting and hovering in their bright colours near the water. Occasionally a big hatch of damselflies will bring trout onto the feed at the surface, often leaping clear to attack them. But underwater the nymph forms a major food item, and the insect predator becomes the prey of fish.

BELOW *Landing a wild rainbow hooked on a dry fly, Frying Pan River, Colorado.*

Imitation points: the dragonfly nymph is a squat, flat, rather beetle-like creature. The damsel nymph is slender and more delicate with distinctive tails. Again the proportions to aim for are two-thirds abdomen, to one-third thorax. Heavily-dubbed bodies are suitable for the dragon-fly nymph, heavily ribbed, with legs of feather fibre or a wind of hackling. The eyes are pronounced and should be imitated with melted nylon blobs or small black beads. Damsel nymphs on the other hand should not be over-dressed. Their slender bodies should be imitated with herl or sparse dubbing, again including a

TOP LEFT A dragonfly nymph, and TOP RIGHT an effective imitation.

ABOVE LEFT A damsel nymph, with, RIGHT, a superb rubber and marabou imitator.

pronounced eye, and a distinctive wingcase. Unlike the dragonfly nymph, the damsel swims sinuously through the water, and part of the abdomen of the artificial is often imitated with a long tail of maribou, or by a detached jointed body. While in their nymphal state the colour range of both creatures is generally brown to olive green.

The adult dragonfly seems to be rarely taken by fish, it is very fast and barely touches the surface. A good adult damsel pattern is simply made by whipping a length of floating fly line, coloured appropriately, onto a hook as a detached body, then dubbing a dark thorax, adding a black cock hackle, and if required, wings of grizzle hackle points. Dragonfly nymphs should be fished in short jerks to imitate their movement, which is performed by expelling jets of water. Movements of 1–3in (2.5–7.6cm) are suitable.

Damsels can be fished in longer steady pulls. Cast near weedbeds,

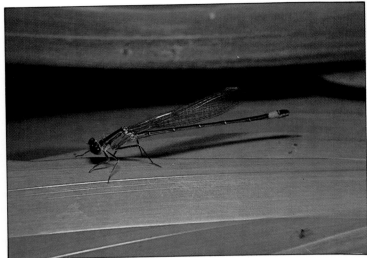

TOP LEFT *A newly
emerged dragonfly atop its
nymphal case, and* TOP RIGHT *a
blue damselfly.*
BOTTOM *A superb catch.*

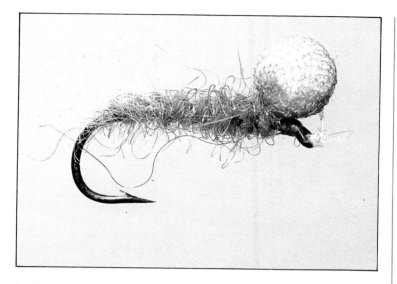

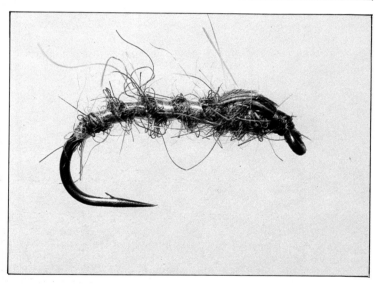

they can be left to sink. In order to hatch, both species crawl up weeds or other features so concentrate on the weedy areas. Hook range, longshank 12 to 8.

DIPTERA

This is probably the single most important family of flies to consider when trout fishing in stillwater, and often in rivers. Diptera include the very important midges (chironomids, often called 'buzzers'), the similar, but biting, mosquitoes, and the craneflies (daddy- or harry-longlegs) and this large subject deserves a book to itself.

TOP LEFT A good midge pupa imitation.
TOP RIGHT A Suspender Buzzer – a midge imitator.
ABOVE LEFT Simplicity in the extreme, a midge pupa from the author's box.
ABOVE RIGHT Contrast this with an equally effective close-copy pupa.

MIDGES Let us consider the typical midge life-cycle, and the imitations the angler can use.

The larval stage (called the blood-worm) lives in the bottom silt, but must frequently emerge or be washed or dug out because trout are often found stuffed with them. The colour ranges from blood red through brown to palest green. They move with a very pronounced wriggle, and good imitations have been made with maribou, dyed chamois, or rubber bands. Another attempt at this effect is to dress the patterns on curbed hooks. Simple wraps of translucent dubbing, ribbed with nylon to imitate the worm-like natural, are deadly; a simple wrap of a transluscent plastic such as larva lace or swan-nundaze is deadly too. Fish the pattern deep and slowly early-season; or higher in the water when weed-beds begin to rot and break up in warm weather. The weeds carry the little

bloodworms, they then drop free for the trout to eat, so a free-falling presentation can be deadly.

The pupa is even higher on the trout's menu. The larvae pupate, and when they emerge from their tunnels, they may hover in deep water for some time. But at hatching time, when the pupa swims vigorously to the surface, the trout take a particular interest. And, like the mayflies, many midge pupae are eaten as they emerge at the surface. Imitations should again be two-thirds abdomen, one-third thorax, the bodies as slender and sparse as possible (even a bare hook will work), and there is seldom any need to copy tiny wing buds, or even the pupa's distinctive breathers, as this only adds bulk. A simple wing case and dubbed thorax usually suffices. A rib or some other indication of segmentation can improve the imitation. For close-copy patterns, wing buds of feather fibre, and sparse breathers of white floss can be incorporated.

The hatching pupa can be dressed with some buoyancy incorporated in the form of foam or dubbing; sparse palmered flies work well too, as does incorporating a shuck (which the golden pheasant tippets of the classic wet flies imitates perfectly). There is a huge colour range in the midge pupa (and like all insects on close examination it is rarely a single colour) and some anglers' experiments have led them to suspect that the colour changes chameleon-like to suit the underwater terrain. But a suitable range is black, brown, green(s), olive green, gold (ivory or tan), amber or orange, red and claret. The adult midge

OPPOSITE Going afloat for a day's lake trouting.

TOP A cranefly, or daddy-longlegs.

ABOVE An effective swamped cranefly imitator.

seems to be rarely taken by fish.

Hook range is vast, with curved and standard shank hooks from 22s up to 8s necessary, plus a few longshank hooks with exaggerated patterns tied on them to stand out in a big hatch.

CRANEFLIES The vast majority of these primitive insects are not aquatic. Occasionally the larva of the terrestrial species finds its way into the water. The larva is creamy, translucent, fat, and caterpillar-shaped, with distinctive segmentation and little else worth imitating. Some varieties swim, so use a plump, dubbed body plus a swimming 'tail' of maribou. The adult is a poor flier, so even terrestrial species get blown onto the water from time to time, where the fish

relish them. The adult is generally dressed as a dry fly, but in recent years the ploy of fishing the crane-fly imitation wet has been very successful, even when there are few craneflies around.

The distinctive dangling legs can be imitated by knotted feather

fibres, or boar bristles, and can be tied splayed-out, or in a dragged bunch. A long, dull-tan body is best constructed of feather fibre, with a dark hackle. Alternatively dispense with the legs and tie in an over-large hackle in a swept-back or parachute style.

STONEFLIES
(ORDER PLECOPTERA)

The stoneflies are at home in fast-flowing, gravel-bottomed streams. These are some of the largest aquatic true flies, some species growing to nearly 3in (7.6cm) long. This makes them very interesting to imitate, for they can be closely copied by any fly dresser with passable eyesight. Bodies are roughly half abdomen and half legs-and-thorax. There are two pronounced tails; strong, distinctively jointed legs, feelers and two wingcases. In colour the nymph varies from dark brown, through creamy gold, to light grey. The adult is like a four-winged version of the nymph, and because of its bulk it is often imitated with deer hair bodies and wings. The colour range is a clear yellow through to golden brown.

The sheer solidity of the nymph means that simple chenille-bodied patterns, with heavy thoraxes, and palmered hackles to copy the legs, score quite well. Alternatively, at the other end of the scale, come immaculate patterns with wingcases formed with wing burner, and carefully knotted jointed legs.

ARTIFICIAL FLIES

DRY FLIES   Virtually every dry fly is tied as an imitation of a food item,

either aquatic or terrestrial. Because the flies must float, they incorporate buoyant materials such as deer hair, plastic foam, high-quality hackles, or water-resistant dubbing. Various water-proofing substances will help to keep them afloat, and water absorbent powders are available to dry them out when they become waterlogged. The exceptions to the imitative rule are dry salmon flies like the Goofus Bug, or Rat Faced MacDougal. Their attraction comes from their wake-making buoyancy.

IMITATION NYMPHS, LARVAE, AND OTHER UNDERWATER FOODS It is impossible to apply general rules to the huge diversity of underwater foods. Having said that, there are a few things to bear in mind. The

TOP LEFT A typical salmon tube fly – a Garry Dog tied on a brass tube to fish deep in big waters.

TOP RIGHT The traditional winged wet

ABOVE LEFT An Atlantic salmon shrimp pattern

ABOVE RIGHT A traditional palmer pattern, the Soldier Palmer, possibly the greatest killer of stillwater trout

dressing of nymphs must always be a compromise between imitation, sparseness, and mobility. In other words it is very rarely necessary to dress plump nymphs and many commercial patterns are badly overdressed. Sparse slim wisps of feather and dubbing are generally better. That said, try to choose dubbings with plenty of transluscence where applicable,

with some movement and life. Few natural insects (as has already been stated) are one colour, but a blend of several colours, so blended mixtures of dubbings are better. Also on the matter of colour, remember that bodies of artificial flies change colour underwater. Dip your flies into a glass of water and check the colours. Never reject the general non-imitative patterns such as traditional spiders, or the classic Woolly Worm. They'll take their share of trout too.

WET FLIES The classic wet fly has a feather fibre wing, tail of feather fibres, and a throat hackle, with a dubbed or tinsel body. Alternatively, it is palmered over its whole body length, and sometimes winged too. In effect there are two types of wet fly – small streamer-

type flies; and insect-type flies, generally resembling a hatching or drowned adult. Again it is easy to overdress such flies, so aim for sparseness in most cases.

STREAMERS Streamers (or lures as they are also known) will catch every fish that the fly fisherman pursues. In various forms they can imitate small fish; or like the classic Atlantic salmon flies, tempt fish into taking. As well as the winged varieties mentioned in the section on prey fish, flies with long, mobile tails of marabou or similar material are also effective. This section would not be complete without a mention of surface lures. These can be deer hair flies to imitate frogs or mice; or balsa or cork Popping Bugs, painted in bright colours and perhaps with 'legs' of rubber or feather hackles.

BELOW This superb salmon took a large spinning lure.

ATLANTIC SALMON FLIES
The vast majority of these conform to the style of wet fly, or streamer. But the very large hooks on which such flies are sometimes tied — up to 3/0 — means that new styles of fly have been developed to get the same length without hooking problems. Two styles are Waddington mounts, a doubled piece of wire with a loop at each end; or tubes of plastic, aluminium, or brass, with the fly dressed on them. Both will accept a treble hook.

THE FLYFISHERMAN'S TACTICS AND TECHNIQUES

The first fly tied to catch a trout was probably a lure – some combination of coloured material placed on a barbed bone and pulled through water too deep for the fisherman to see and spear his quarry. There is little doubt now that more members of the Salmonid family as well as other game fish fall for wet flies, lures, streamers, and imitations of small fish and other non-insect aquatic creatures, than rise to a dry fly or suck in a nymph imitation.

So in considering the tactics of the modern fly fisherman the first priority is the wet fly. Indeed, when it comes to the migratory fish, few anglers will look further, especially in Europe. But the term 'wet fly' is in itself not ideal, for it does not begin to describe the diversity of methods involved.

Secondly, there is the so-called dry fly: no fly is ever entirely dry once cast to a fish. The method is steeped in centuries of tradition, and is often thought the most challenging technique in the sport. Most non-anglers' vision when imagining the average participant in the sport is the dry fly fisherman. Yet the techniques of dry fly are being brought rapidly up to date. And it must be said that on its day it can be the easiest of methods.

Like the dry fly, fishing the nymph demands a knowledge and method beyond the mere physical skills of casting to or spotting trout. The nymph man is usually an amateur entomologist and very often a fly dresser too.

But the truly great fly fisherman will have a knowledge of, skill at, and take pleasure in each and every legitimate branch of the sport. If he does not he is missing a great deal.

TROUT TACTICS USING WET FLY, STREAMER AND LURE

RIVERS The traditional method of fishing the wet fly for trout in any size of river was to cast a wet fly or team of wet flies across the current and to let them swing around on the stream. A floating, sinking, or sink-tip line might be required depending on the depth of the water and the holding place of the trout. The team might consist of attractors, flashers, or small fish imitators – wet flies with tinsel bodies and wings like the Peter

Fishing for grayling on the River Lambourn.

Ross, or Teal, Blue and Silver; or more insect-like patterns like the Mallard and Claret, or Greenwell's Glory; or of traditional spider patterns, more like modern nymphs in their naturalistic way.

The flies might be allowed to create a wake on the surface such as scurrying caddis, or they might be fished deeper in the water. When they had swung round below the angler, they would be retrieved, and takes often came while the flies were stripped back, then held on the surface, dibbled each in turn, to make a wake like an insect hatching on the surface.

This deadly, traditional method is still widely practised, and works well. The angler can thoroughly cover each pool or run by casting at a different angle each time, by allowing less or more sinking time, and by walking or wading gradu-

ally downstream to cover all available water. He can slow the passage of his flies by throwing an upstream mend into the line (by lifting off line and flicking it back without moving the tip of the fly line), and he can speed up the passage of the fly line by stripping in a little line as the flies come round in the water.

All-in-all it is an adaptable method which has stood the test of time. Probably it works so well because it brings the fly round in a curve. Again and again you will see that this round-the-corner movement, be it through the horizontal or the vertical plane, proves irresistible to trout and many other game fish. Look out for it as the chapter proceeds.

This downstream-and-across wet-fly method brings both a round-the-bend swing, and an up-

ward curve into play, as the angler has the facility to lift the rod, and consequently the flies with it at any stage of fishing them through.

All basic wet fly and streamer river fishing is practised in this way, though of course it is not a method for seeking out fish in specific holes and small pools among the rocks. Such fish will either call for an accurate cast, allowing the fly to sweep through a tight arc in the vicinity of the fish, a leaded fly, or an alternative method such as nymph or dry fly.

The man who seeks large brown trout with imitations of prey fish will use exactly the same method with his Muddler Minnow. As we shall see, the salmon angler adopts similar tactics, and the man in pursuit of steelhead will let his egg pattern swing in exactly the same fashion.

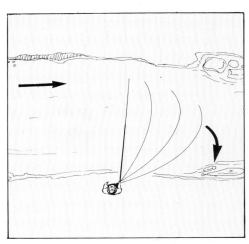

ABOVE A typical river fishing scenario, casting downstream and across. The line sweeps round, its speed governed by the angler's retrieve. In this situation there may well be fish lying in or among the rocks.

RIGHT Casting across and down in pursuit of sea trout. The venue is Scotland's River Spey – home of superb Atlantic salmon.

ABOVE A delightful time – the boat fisher at anchor enjoys the dusk rise.

STILLWATER Wet flies and lures can be treated quite separately on stillwater. Tactics for fishing leach patterns, streamers, and muddlers can be identical to those used for fishing wet flies – but that is the sport at its simplest. There are infinite style variations from the bank, depending on the target fish and the flies used. From a boat, there are as many again. Infinite? Well, yes, in the sense that each little nuance of retrieve, choice of fly, choice of line sinking speed, casting direction, and distance, must be coupled with a powerful sense of what is happening underwater. True in all methods? Perhaps, but the wet fly is the great prospecting method on a new water or when fish refuse to show, cannot be seen, in deep water, and when they refuse to rise. Nine times out of ten the wet fly and

streamer man is fishing 'blind'.

To return to the traditional wet fly method from the bánk. Historically, of course, it is all things to all fish. A stillwater wet fly may be purely a flashing attractor of fish, slightly or definitely insect-like, or tied to imitate a small fish. The classic method with these flies was to tie on three or more, mixing and matching such flies to form a team. If the fish did not take the end or point fly, it might fall to one of the droppers. Up to five flies might be used, though three is normal. Casts were short and frequent, with the flies worked more by raising the rod than any pulling on the line. This of course produced that deadly curve – upward in this case – though as casts were often made across the wind, a sideways curve would tend to be put into the line as well.

At the end of the retrieve, the flies would be held on the surface each in turn, just as if they were hatching insects, and dibbled before being rolled off. The angler would then take a pace to his side and repeat the cast. Miles of bank could be covered in a day and almost inevitably the angler would make his bag of wild brown trout. Like all the great traditional styles, the method still works today and will often be seen in use in Wales and Scotland on the llyns and lochs.

These waters were invariably deep in the middle, with little available food away from the margins where the trout always lay. Faced with other more challenging waters, with fish more inclined to cruise than to hold in shallow bankside waters, a wider range of tactics is called for.

ABOVE the author's simple dressing of a leach-style pattern can also be fished as a lure.

Prospecting a large stillwater that might contain good brown trout, rainbows, and perhaps brook trout, might call for longer casting, and a method that will cover different depths efficiently. Teams of wet flies are best not cast long distances, and the choice will lie between a single wet fly or small streamer, or something more imitative. The presence in one form or another of prey fish for the trout might provide a guideline.

If in doubt, a simple black or white streamer pattern, or a leaded black or brown leach-style pattern will be a useful first choice. Local favourites should never be ignored, of course, but whatever the fly, a basic prospecting technique is essential. In the absence of easily observed surface movement, the best bet will probably be a medium-sinking

line, possibly a shooting-head for maximum distance. If you know the water is very deep, a fast-sinker might be a better choice.

With no fish to be seen on the surface, the depth at which they are feeding must be found. If they are located, a wet fly or streamer lure will at least draw taps and follows, even from disinterested fish. So the aim is to cover the water thoroughly by fan casting — that is making each cast a few degrees further round an imaginary arc in front of us — and by counting down the fly line as it sinks.

With the excellent modern fly lines an angler will know exactly how deep the line is after 20 seconds. But that knowledge is irrelevant if a note has not been made of how far the line has sunk when a fish has been hooked. So, first time round the arc, allow a count of five sinking time, then ten, twenty, and so on until the bottom is snagged. If a fish takes at a particular moment, repeat the angle of the cast (it could be that the angle of the light was important) and allow the same sinking time. What actually happens is that you do not actually count but you do develop a feel for searching the water — and you do tend to remember the correct angle of cast even if you forget how deep your line was.

Another complication is speed of retrieve. With a floating line you could simply let your fly be blown round by the wind. With a sinker you have to pull it back. This can be done at any speed from barely moving (in which case remember that fly and line are still slowly sinking), to a supersonic strip that makes a blurr of your left hand.

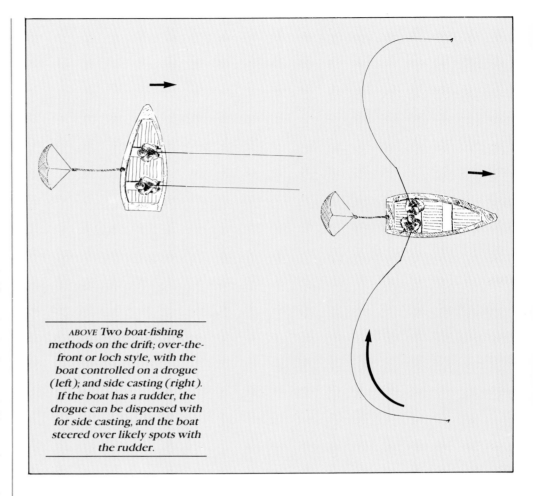

ABOVE *Two boat-fishing methods on the drift; over-the-front or loch style, with the boat controlled on a drogue (left); and side casting (right). If the boat has a rudder, the drogue can be dispensed with for side casting, and the boat steered over likely spots with the rudder.*

Add to this the differences in tempo: are you making your fly twitch and limp like a wounded prey fish? Are you jigging your lead-headed leach back sink and draw, or allowing your muddler pattern to pause and float buoyantly upward like a wounded minnow, or is it simply whizzing back to you like a torpedo? All is far from simple. Now add a further complication. How can you get that deadly curve into your retrieve? Simple — cast out and take a couple of steps sideways before retrieving. Now you have that curve. In virtually all types of fly fishing, never snatch off a cast at the end of the retrieve. Always slowly lift the rod and hold the fly in the surface, looking at every stage of the retrieve for a following fish. If a fish does come up fast behind the fly, it pays on most occasions to keep the fly moving. When you can retrieve no further, use the length of the rod, and sweep the fly away to one side or the other. By this means that deadly curve will be produced again and very often it induces a take, sometimes right under the feet. In fact, in streamer lure fishing the angler should expect to take as many as a third of his fish on the final lift. Always make one, even when there is no sight of the fly or of any fish.

RETRIEVES Stripping back a fly is standard practice when wet fly or streamer fishing. The best way to do this is to hold the rod low after casting, and adopt one of two methods, either pointing straight at the fly to feel and hook takes, or

at a slight angle to cushion against getting smashed by a hard take. Retrieve line with the left hand after hooking it under the index finger of the right hand. When a take is felt, the finger clamps down on the line to act as a brake, and the rod is lifted. Just how firm all these motions should be, comes with practice. Stripping-in line need not be fast, or in smooth, successive pulls, it can also be very slow, or jerky and limping like an injured prey fish.

WET FLY FROM A BOAT All the streamer lure methods will work almost equally well with wet flies, but there is a great traditional method of wet fly fishing that equates closely to the short-line from the bank. A team of carefully chosen flies, usually three or four, are tied onto a cast, and the boat is arranged broadside on at the top of a likely drift. That is an area of water downwind likely to hold trout. The boat may be slowed by a drogue – underwater 'parachute' – but is otherwise at the mercy of the wind. The angler, or more often anglers at either end of the boat, cast more or less straight down the wind (and, as they become more experienced, to either side of the boat), and retrieve at a speed which will vary with the speed of drift. Sometimes quite a fast retrieve will barely move the flies in the water.

The distance cast traditionally was very short – hence the old name of shortlining. Modern anglers will cast further, but if they are wise they will remain seated while they do it, because the beauty of this method is the visual aspect, and the chance to draw up fish from the depths to follow right up to the boat before taking the fly, which once again must be held and dibbled on the surface. The choice for the top dropper is very often a palmered fly, one with a hackle wound the full length of the body,

which wakes across the surface, drawing fish up to the top. The skill often lies in not pulling the fly away from a chasing fish, but allowing it to simply close its mouth on it, or more excitingly roll over the fly where a delayed lift of the rod is necessary to set the hook. Floating lines are traditionally employed for this method, which is at its most exciting over shallow water, on the traditional lakes and lochs where it developed, or where there are shoals of fish moving down the wind.

With two anglers casting all around the arc in front of the boat, large areas of water can be covered thoroughly. There is also an argument for very long rods for this method –from 11–16ft (3.3–4.8m) which gives the angler the chance to lift the rod and dibble the flies farther from the boat, and with less chance of frightening a following fish. Again the method employs that deadly upward curve.

SIDE CASTING On this occasion, not the side cast employed to get a fly into an awkward spot, but casting sideways from a drifting boat.

Dibbling the top dropper is an art. The expert, lifting his rod and drawing the fly across the water in a smooth sweep, not only pulls fish up to his top dropper, but entices them to devour other flies on the cast.

In this method the boat is set up to drift downward bows first, either by the intelligent use of a rudder, or less efficiently with a drogue over the stern, although this removes some of the steerability of the boat.

Here the angler, or anglers, again at opposite sides of the boat, but most often standing in the bows, cast out sideways and, as the boat drifts, allow their lines to curve round naturally in the water, retrieving only as the line straightens, or if they feel the fish want a fast-moving fly. Most takes come as the line is almost straight behind the boat and the fly comes round the bend.

Quite deep water can be searched thoroughly by utilising the full range of sinking lines. The anglers can also effectively employ floating lines, and leaded, or wake-making flies.

Usually the anglers will employ streamers or leach-style patterns, and some very large flies can be successful. The most extreme version of the method is the use of very powerful rods, shooting-heads of lead-cored trolling line, and a method best described as wind-trolling or trailing, where the angler does not retrieve when his fly comes around behind the boat, but, boringly, allows it to trail behind. Quite large lakes can be searched thoroughly with the method, which has been employed where 'fly tackle only' is the rule. But the method scarcely qualifies as fly fishing. Often, any semblance of fly casting is forgotten and the tackle just dropped over the back.

The beauty of true side casting is that headlands, shallows, islands, and weedbeds can all be searched thoroughly while the boat is rudder controlled.

FISHING A SINKING LINE The importance of counting down the line has been stressed, and fishing the full range of sinking lines to cover all likely depths of water, as well as the fact that you must mix up your retrieves. Takes to a floating line are often visual — but while you may see an underwater flash when a fish takes a sunk fly, what the angler mostly feels is a pull, pure and simple. Very often the fish hooks itself against the inertia of the line. Sometimes it won't, and you must pull back against the most delicate of takes. Just to confuse the issue, other fish will tap away and never be hooked. Recently stocked fish are a typical example and the European sea trout is another. Every fish that ever took a fly will have days when it will pluck and days when it takes. There are a number of solutions to this. The first method is to ignore the taps and keep fishing, when, very often, the fish will hook itself. Speeding up the retrieve often works, or just stopping the retrieve for a moment, then whipping the fly away in imitation of a wounded creature stunned, then trying to swim away.

Rarely, stopping the retrieve completely will induce a take and, even more unusually, slowing down the retrieve to 'let the fish

RIGHT *The great journey continues, as a leaping salmon confronts the full power of a waterfall.*

catch the fly' as one novice put it, will bring results. Try them all, and also try sharpening your hook! At the other extreme come smash takes, for there is a lot of inertia in a sinking line, and a fish hitting your fly hard may smash the leader before you can react.

If it happens often, try the simple trick of angling your rod away from the line to create a cushion. Better still, take those two sideways steps and put that deadly curve in your line, to cushion the takes, and probably bring you a few extra fish.

At any rate, it often pays to fish a little heavier when using a sunken line – 8lb (3.6kg) where 5lb (2.2kg) would usually suffice, perhaps. Never try to lift too much sunken line out of the water, the old books will tell you that you will break your rod. With a modern carbon rod this is possible but unlikely. More likely is that you will get the line whipping back and hitting you in the face, a hook in your ear, or at the least a monumental tangle.

Remember the chapter on tackle; your rod is designed to lift off the correct weight of line, not that same line made heavy by the 'friction' of water on it. So, fish out your cast, including the final lift, and the holding of the fly near the surface, then roll off your line, and go smoothly into the back cast.

DRY FLY

For some anglers this is the most difficult of methods, others the easiest. If we take the dry fly to mean fishing an insect imitation at the water's surface, then we can include several of the methods mentioned in the nymphing section of this chapter. On the other hand, if we say it is fishing an imitation of an adult fly or terrestrial near the surface, without retrieving it, we do at least differentiate between the wet fly and the nymph method. That said, no experienced dry-fly man would like to be told that he must never move his fly, even in imitation of something like a caddis, which

LEFT Working up the Eagle River, Colorado, deep-wading and casting a dry fly.

OPPOSITE Up goes the rod and a fish battles in the Frying Pan River, Colorado.

often skims across the top as it attempts to leave the water, or a cranefly, which can set up a struggle that demands a twitched imitation to approach a life-like presentation.

But that initial picture – a fly cast out, left to float, and simply watched by the angler until a fish pushes up its nose and engulfs it, could suggest to anyone the idea that dry fly is easy.

Another image, that of the selective trout (which on the many catch-and-release waters are becoming more common) carefully refusing all but the perfect imitation floated over it, on a gossamer tippet, and immaculately presented, might also give the impression that this is the most difficult style of all. Then add to

this the extraordinary British cult of dry-fly-only on the great chalk-streams, and dry fly can take on a mystique that it hardly deserves.

Most members of the trout family are uniquely equipped for surface feeding. Even their eyes have evolved to be more efficient for this than bottom grubbing. Therefore it makes sense to fish a dry fly now and again, when the method is suitable. But it should never become the be all and end all. It is not the only method worthy of respect. It is another weapon in the fly fisherman's armoury.

RIVERS Dry fly in rivers has been hidebound by tradition. There is a lot to be said for up-stream dry fly. It is in fact the simplest method of putting a dry fly over the majority

of river fish. But there are wild streams where such an approach, however time-honoured, is neither necessary, nor the best approach. Generally on these waters, it is a question of presenting a fly to a trout by any possible method. Where the rules permit, getting a fly over a trout without scaring it with bad casts, or the sight of a leader, or definitely of a fly line, should be done in whichever way possible. Up-stream fishing was the good old British chalkstream tradition, and like many traditions it was founded on common sense.

Suppose you spot a confidently feeding trout and want to put your fly over it. Getting down-stream and casting up-river and slightly across, should mean that only your fly and the minimum amount of your nylon leader (degreased to sink) will pass through the trout's 'window', as it watches the passing stream of food. Should the fish not rise to your offering, your fly and line can float on down the river and be retrieved without disturbing it. Then imagine the same scene casting down-stream. The fly floats down, and once again the trout sees only the fly and leader. Then unfortunately the fly line may well follow. The alternative to the fly line drifting over the fish may be to lift off quickly and create a splash that may scare the trout. Of course this won't be the case from all effective angles, but from many you will at least have to show the fish the fly line.

There is at least one situation where you might succeed with this method. Drifting a caddis, or possibly a fish imitator, or perhaps a small muddler over a trout, then pulling it smoothly back up-stream, may give your fly the semblance of life. You can then strip the fly and line back clear of the trout before casting. Mostly, though, it is essential to float your dry fly at a dead drift over the trout. Any suspicion of drag or unnatural movement will generally put the trout off. This means that casting tricks, like the ability to throw a snakey line and leader which will gradually straighten out under the pull of a contradictory current, are essential.

RISES – AND HOW TO HOOK THEM It is possible to spot a trout that is apparently not feeding, put a dry fly over it and hook it. Mostly, the dry-fly fisherman casts to fish observed rising to flies passing overhead. But to hook these fish several abilities are needed that have

ABOVE How not to play a leaping fish. Undecided, the angler has neither dropped the rod, nor kept it up to cushion the leap. This angler risks both a fine rainbow straight-lining him, and, losing the spring of the rod, breaking his leader.

nothing at all to do with casting skill, or control of tackle. First, not all 'rising' fish are taking flies off the surface. Often their choice is nymphs that are on their way to hatch at the surface; at other times they take the 'still-born' – nymphs that fail to hatch and are glued in the surface film. The trout may not even be feeding on aquatic flies but terrestrial insects; worse still, they have been known to take other objects, such as wind blown seeds or even feathers.

A second skill, then, is to observe what the trout are taking. Sometimes, during a huge hatch, it is obvious that on other occasions more than a single insect species may be available with the trout selecting just one. Worse still, it may be selecting just one stage of the hatching cycle of the insect concerned. The dry-fly man really does need a smattering of entomology!

When a trout rises, it does so in a variety of ways from a tiny kiss at the surface to a full-blooded lashing splash. Hooking these rises is not always easy. They demand different timing, varying from an instant reaction to a delay of a second or more, before lifting. Generally, the larger the fly, the longer the pause. A trout engulfing a cranefly might demand a good full 'God save the Queen', spoken out loud and pompously before the angler dare lift to set the hook. A trout sipping-in a tiny chironomid or mosquito can require an instant response. A fish used to snatching its food from the surface of a fast-flowing stream will react more quickly than one that feeds leisurely in a deep slow pool.

There is no doubt that patience is the secret when attempting to set the hook – it is rare that a fast lift is necessary. The grayling is one definite exception; this widespread game fish can demand reactions like greased lightning. But then the grayling is a freak surface feeder – its underslung mouth is all wrong for the job.

STILLWATER Patience is always a virtue, and the stillwater man often needs it in vast quantities. Quite often he will be casting to rising fish. But when he is not, there is no river current to wash away the fly, ready for him to cast again. Instead, he has to sit awaiting the boil of a fish coming up from the depths, which can happen at any time, and usually does while he is drinking his coffee or a cool beer. Of course, on most days drift will bring the fly back to the bank, and the angler will cast again. He may choose, though, to get the wind behind him, and let his floating line gradually drift out to search more water. This way a whole fly line and some backing can be released – then try to lift it off to set the hook in a trout!

Another more accurate method is to cast out with a side wind, and to walk along the bank, mending line by flicking it forwards, letting the fly go along on a natural drift. Good areas of bank can be covered this way, and plenty of water. Another mobile method is to set a boat broadside on and cast a dry fly out in front, staying in touch with the fly, or team of flies, by gently retrieving just enough line so as not to move the fly. When you come up on the fly you cast again. One often encounters very good hatches of caddis flies on stillwater, and then the dry fly can be mobile. An elk or deer-hair caddis pattern can be gently waked back across the surface and palmered flies are also deadly in this role.

RISES It is likely that the stillwater dry-fly man will be casting farther than the river angler. There is a lot of stretch in a standard fly line and in addition it resists being pulled from the surface tension of the water. So the stillwater dry-fly man will often have to react more firmly, and sometimes faster than the river man. At long range, it is better to set the hook with a sideways, not an upwards, sweep of

the rod. This will tend to slide the line across the surface instead of pulling it off.

NYMPHING

For the purposes of this book, 'nymphing' is the technique of fishing for trout with an imitation of any underwater trout food except a prey-fish imitator. Crustacea such as scuds and shrimps, gastropods such as snails and leeches – none of these are aquatic *insects*. Strictly speaking nymphing should apply only to the nymphs of underwater aquatic flies – the sub-aquatic stage between larva and imago or adult. But again, leaning on the British chalkstream tradition, nymphing is a satis-factory expression for fishing imitations of these foods.

RIVERS British tradition would again make the up-stream cast the only proper way to fish a nymph. Even greater respectability could be obtained by casting only to a fish that is seen to be feeding. We need not restrict ourselves this way, unless fishery rules insist. But it follows from this that a nymphing trout – one feeding on underwater food forms – may be easily spotted. Of course, if the trout is rising to near-surface food forms, it may easily be mistaken for a fish taking the dry fly. The signs can be easily observed deeper in the water, clarity permitting. Generally a busily feeding river trout will be 'on the fin', its body swaying from

RIGHT The legendary British angler, Hugh Falkus, pursues salmon on the Cumbrian Esk in northern England. Note the rod held low, and the loose line for the salmon to take.

side to side in the current, mouthing at the food as it passes. This wink of white in the water, as the trout's white inner mouth flashes, is unmistakable, and often a useful semaphore for the angler.

Occasionally a trout will be observed nudging and nuzzling the weed, to flush out food. Other times the fish will stand on its head to take food from the bottom. The signs are clear and while an apparently non-feeding trout may move to your nymph, a bristling trout is eminently catchable.

Visible trout are what nymphing is all about. The aim is to approach that fish with a reasonable imitation of what it is feeding on, presented in a natural fashion. Upstream is an excellent way to do

BELOW The induced take. It is imperative to get the nymph down to the correct depth, then to lift the fly as it nears the fish's nose.

this, the fish is lying facing away from the angler, and with a good cast, the nymph can be dunked onto the water up-stream of its nose, with only a small part of the leader visible.

It is important to judge two things when casting: the distance past the fish that will allow the nymph to sink sufficiently to arrive in the fish's vision at just the right depth and the allowance of sufficient slack in the line and leader for any conflicting current that might whisk away the nymph before it reaches the fish.

So not only must the angler choose a reasonable imitation of what is hatching, or likely to be drifting along the river, he must also be sure that the imitation is adequately loaded to sink to the fish in the time allowed. Weight with copper wire, lead foil or wire, or occasionally lead weights applied separately to the leader.

A fly could be left to trickle into the trout's mouth on a dead drift, and the fish might take it. But if it does not, the induced-take lift

should be tried. Again, utilize that deadly upward curve by giving a pull on the line or lifting the rod when we think the fly is in the vicinity of the trout.

If the trout is visible, there are several clues to it taking your imitation. You may be able to see that classic opening or closing of the mouth, a flash of white. You may see the fish open and shut its mouth as if it is trying to crush the fly. It may sway violently or smoothly to left or right in order to intercept the fly. It may also tip up on its tail or nose to reach for your artificial.

But if these are tell-tale visual signs, there are other signals visible above the water. You can grease the leader, and watch that for pauses or stops. You can watch the fly line tip for jerks or stops, fix a strike indicator to your line, or leader, which will function like the bait fisherman's float or bobber, diving under if a fish (or a piece of weed, or other snag) touches your fly. There are, too, commercial fly lines available with an integral sight bulb in the tip.

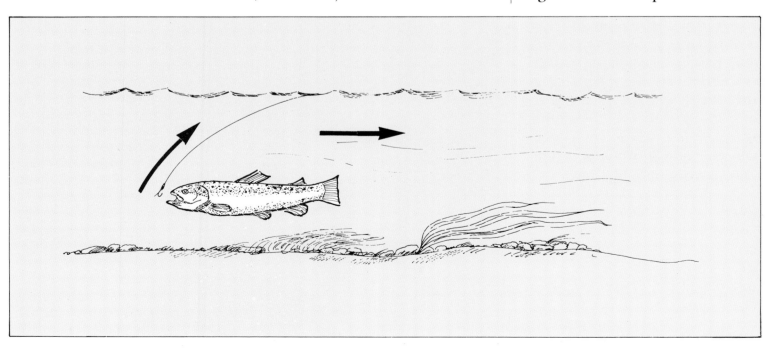

FISHING BLIND The same techniques can be applied to deep holes and pots where the fish are not visible. Sometimes it is possible to get very close to the fish, and without casting, simply lower the heavily leaded nymph into the water and work it down-stream with the rod tip, lifting to induce takes when the fly seems handily placed, and constantly in touch through the rod tip. You must of course both look and feel for takes.

OTHER PRESENTATIONS Where the method is allowed, there is no reason why you should not cast down-stream with the nymph. One method is similar to the up-stream visual technique, letting the fly drift down to the fish ahead of the line and leader, and simply stopping its drift, and producing a take-inducing lift from the nymph as it arrives at the trout's nose.

Alternatively, one can simply fish the nymph in the river wet-fly fashion, as described earlier in the chapter. In extreme conditions, a sinking line could be used with this technique to get a fly right down. Takes would have to be felt for, and it is only a method for fast water where the flow forces a fish to act quickly, and perhaps take more firmly.

HATCHING NYMPHS So far it has been assumed that the angler is approaching a fish lying deep in the water. It is worth remembering that feeding area between out-and-out dry fly, and the dead-drifted nymph. Of course, part of the reason that the deadly upward curve applied when inducing a take is so effective is that it resembles a nymph beginning its journey to the top to hatch at the water surface.

ABOVE Pot-shooting may not be legal everywhere, unless it is performed upstream as in the diagram. Here the length of the rod, a long leader, and a heavily weighted nymph combine to put the fly on the fish's nose under the control of the rod. Casting is not involved – the fly is dunked in and controlled by the rod tip.

BELOW Playing a Frying Pan brown trout. This one took a nymph.

RIGHT To fish nymphs really slowly on a side wind the angler simply casts out and lets the wind sweep the floating line round. He retrieves as necessary. Alternatively, with nymph or dry fly, he can mend line and move along the bank with the wind, giving his fly a steady drift and covering more water.

BELOW RIGHT This brown trout shows the typical bronze of the out-of-season fish, and is going back to be caught in the spring.

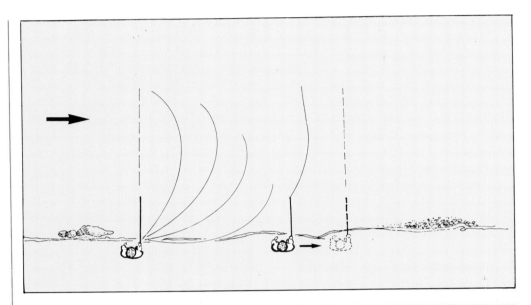

general imitative duties, probably on a short shank No. 10 or 8 hook with the tail clipped accordingly short.

Droppers should also be used, as the point fly, which is always leaded, will be fished slow and deep and pick up a lot of weed. Natural droppers are midge pupae imitations, or perhaps early may-flies — olives as they are known in Europe.

Most of the midges are slow swimmers so they lend themselves best to these techniques. A floating line is the most useful weapon, with a two dropper cast. The angler then has several choices, if a warmer-than-the-water wind is blowing he may choose to face in-to it, as it will push food and warmer surface water down on the undertow, and gather trout. If there is an icy wind, the warmer water will be found where the wind is on his back. A side wind, left to right for a right hander, is ideal for fishing the flies. So when the angler picks a head or back wind, for best effect he will turn half sideways and cast across it.

So, with the cast made at an angle to the wind, the angler simply allows his fly team to sink, then allows the wind to pull the line around, achieving a natural

drift, and a perfect, slow, steady re-trieve. A stopping or moving of the fly line indicates a take, when the angler should not attempt to lift off the line to set the hook, but must move the rod sideways, parallel to the water surface, which slides the line along and sets the hook.

With a good left to right wind an additional trick is to mend line with forward flicks and walk the flies along the bank for as far as possible — covering more water.

Even this slow, wind-assisted retrieve will actually move a cased caddis larva far faster than the natural could move, but it is close to something the trout will accept. Besides, the point fly is often 'sacrificial' in that it acts as a little

anchor for the other flies.

One could also cast down-wind a fair distance and make a slow figure-of-eight or coiled-hand retrieve, but this requires more skill and patience. Equally, to fish deep you could use a sinking line, and if one suspects that fish are in water of over 20ft (6m) deep it will be the only choice. But a sinking line means that you have to retrieve faster to keep your flies out of the bottom snags.

As the water warms, it is possible to use a similar method to fish higher in the water. By carefully retrieving a little line you can fish your flies at all depths, and locate feeding fish. However, the mayflies/olives can get up a fair speed, and it often pays to fish their imitations quite swiftly, especially when the odd natural fly is seen hatching, and nymphs are moving to the surface with their tail-lashing swim. The retrieve then is a series of slow steady 1-ft (0.3-m) strips.

Members of the caddis family are not good swimmers, and their clumsy take-off attempts at the surface, once they have hatched, mean that their nymphal imitations can quite effectively be fished in quick strips on occasions.

Classic summer evening rises can be incredibly difficult, with trout everywhere, and perhaps more than one species of insect hatching at the same time. With a huge amount of food lodged in the surface film, and many more nymphs moving upwards, the trout may want the flies absolutely static in the surface film, or sped along 2ft (0.6m) down.

If the fish 'want' static flies, then it may be necessary to use a de-

greased leader and nymphs with built-in buoyancy, or sometimes a sunken dry fly; or maybe to grease-up and leave everything absolutely still so that the nylon creates no surface wake. The first method is almost always preferable. It might be possible to work through the rising fish with a steady retrieve and catch several of them. But it may need some extra inducement, such as casting near a moving fish and stripping the nymph or nymphs away – the 'GT midge' as it is sometimes called!

Through the season, the nymph man needs to carry a full range of imitations in his fly box; to recognise the flies in the air and on the water; and to use a marrow spoon on dead trout, or possibly a snake

bite syringe on live ones to identify exactly what the fish is feeding on. Often it will be a range of items, but when fish are concentrated on a particular nymph, the angler will be hard pressed to take it on an imitation of anything else.

Some quick tips. In a big hatch, try a correctly sized imitation first.

If that does not work try an exaggeration – perhaps a longshank version of the same hook size – something that will stand out from the mass of flies.

Sometimes it pays to try a different colour, or to incorporate a dash of fluorescent material into the imitation. For instance, fluorescent green seems to have a special appeal to rainbow trout in stillwater. Another tip is not to neglect general patterns. Among the classics are the Gold Ribbed Hare's Ear nymph, the Black (hackled) and Peacock (bodied) Spider, the Half Back nymph, or the classic Woolly Worm. These are universal patterns, and will often secure a fish that on investigation will give a clue to the diet of the others.

ABOVE A rainbow captured on dry fly is eased to hand on a superb American river.

DEADLY VARIATIONS

There are dozens of ways of catching trout on fly tackle for which there is no room in this work. But no round-up would be complete without mentioning some deadly variations on the various themes.

PREY-FISH FEEDERS Today's imitative-minded angler will carry some good small-fish imitations. Some of these could almost be called close-copy patterns. He will also have a good range of standard streamers which have fish-like qualities, but there are certain circumstances where the angler would apparently be certain of scoring with these flies – and yet he rarely does.

It happens mainly on stillwater when a shoal of game fish work together to herd small prey-fish into the margins and weedbeds. The trout then come in on raids slashing at the mass of fry indiscriminately, perhaps catching one or two, but wounding many more. These crippled fish tend to come to the top, where the game fish return to pick them up. It can be frustrating to fish for these 'fry feeders' because your fish imitator is one among hundreds, and is more likely to be taken while sinking than while making a steady journey back to the end of your rod. There is a solution that often works, it is to throw a floating pattern into the area of the disturbance.

A standard muddler works well, but better patterns are tied of translucent foam, clipped to a fish shape. It is usually very important to match the length of the bait-fish, but otherwise the method is easy. You cast the fly into the area of activity, and allow it to float until

ABOVE Flies from the author's own box; a Floating Fry pattern – the curved hook imitates the dead natural at the surface (top); a heavily-hackled dapping fly (middle); a Booby – the polystyrene beads at the head give it deadly bouyancy (bottom).

taken, or until it drifts away from the effective area. Retrieving the pattern with a series of slow twitches can also work, but mostly it needs to be static. If a fish takes the fly, pause a little longer than you would for a standard dry fly, then set the hook. Sometimes a trout will nuzzle the fly without taking, and it can pay to slowly ease the fly away from the fish, when it will often take. Alternatively, squeeze the fly in the water. A little moisture in the foam puts it in, rather than on, the surface film and can make a difference.

Strangely, it is always worth casting a cranefly imitation or perhaps an elk hair or deer hair caddis into the mêlée. With the feeding trout looking for tasty morsels, perhaps it is seen as an easy offering.

DAPPING Dapping is a classic method of presenting a fly without scaring a trout. You simply let the wind do the work. If you make up a blow line from four or five strands of 2lb (0.9kg) nylon knotted every 3ft (0.9m), and about 12ft (3.6m) long overall, you will find that it streams out in a good wind, and, most usually on stillwater and from a boat, you can drift along just holding your fly suspended on the water. Between it and the blow line you can have as little as 3ft (0.9m) of quite heavy nylon, because in dapping the line should never touch the water.

Flies for dapping are often large and well-hackled, and the method takes trout, sea trout, and salmon on the British lakes, lochs, and loughs. From a tree-lined or bushy bank the river angler can employ a

LEFT As there is no casting involved in dapping, three rods can fish together in this boat on Lough Ennell, southern Ireland.

similar technique on awkward fish by sneaking up on them through the available cover, and lowering his fly (dry or even nymph) steadily onto the fish where it lies.

BUOYANT FLY/SUNK LINE Whether in the early season cold, or in heat-wave conditions deep-lying fish are a problem. They may want a fly very close to the bottom, in 20ft (6m) of water. How do you fish that far down, and slowly, without snagging? The answer lies in a combination of a fast-sinking line and a buoyant fly, joined by a short leader. In tests in the UK, it has been found that as little as 6in (15cm) between the fly and the fly line can still produce takes.

A more usual leader length is about 3ft (0.9m). With a muddler or, far better, a fly with a body of sealed plastic foam, the angler can cast out, let the line sink right

down to the bottom, then slowly work his pattern back very close to the bottom. There seems to be a certain seduction in the up and down motion of the flies and their stop-start action that trout love, and there is no reason why a longer leader and droppers should not be used. Midges are especially good in this role, as they rise vertically from the bottom, lifted by the buoyant point fly. The line must be watched where it enters the water and when the angler is not retrieving it offers an excellent indication of a take. Again, don't try to lift the sunk line out of the water. Set the hook by pulling back with the left hand – then lift the rod.

In the UK, a whole range of flies have been designed for this method. Known as the Booby series, they have twin 'eyes' of expanded polystyrene foam encased

in stocking material. These make the flies buoyant, and, as an added sideline, give it a swaying action in the water. The inventor was the well-known nymph angler and professional fly dresser Gordon Fraser of Melton Mowbray, Leicestershire.

Incidentally, the Bass Bug can be effective for trout in this role, having both buoyancy and a good action in the water.

SALMON FISHING

The Atlantic salmon and its Pacific cousins are mainly fished for using standard river techniques, with large wet flies, and in the case of the Pacific fish, with egg-imitating flies. There can be no doubt that the increasing scarcity of, and temperament of the Atlantic salmon makes it the more challenging and difficult fish. So we shall examine some twists of standard wet-fly fishing that may lead to its capture.

In early season and in big waters, the salmon may require fast-sinking lines, and big brass-bodied tube flies, up to 3in (7.6cm) long. Also popular are the Waddington mounts, a doubled length of wire with a loop at each end, which has a treble hook at the tail, and over which the fly is dressed. Later, smaller flies will score, in sizes 1/0 down to 10s or 12s, which must be increasingly

ABOVE *This nose-hooked Atlantic salmon from the Tweed may have been struck a little soon – the angler was lucky to get a good hook hold in such a boney area of the mouth.*

sparsely dressed as the water clears and lowers. Floating lines come in, and salmon may be persuaded to lift to a fly just below the surface in just a few feet (a metre) of water.

Standard wet-fly tactics are employed, but as has been mentioned, the long rod may still be used – up to 18ft (5.4m) or more – to add to the control of the fly at long range on a big river. The fly will also be allowed to swing round at the end of its drift, and be held for some time over a likely lie while 'on the dangle'. It will then be stripped back with care, and on occasions this produces fish. At other times the fly is simply lifted off and cast again.

DRY FLY Only in recent years has the European angler come to realize that the dry fly will take salmon. There have always been accidents, and the stories are manifold of good salmon that rose

to, and took, perhaps, a big dry mayfly, but few anglers have fished for salmon deliberately this way. Yet in the US the technique is well-known and honoured; and on the sea lochs and loughs of Scotland and Ireland, salmon have always risen to large dapped dry flies. (In passing it should be added that standard over-the-front wet-fly tactics are the more usual way of pursuing the 'stillwater' salmon and sea trout.)

Some anglers will tell you that only the salmon of certain rivers will respond to the method, yet the salmon in the East coast rivers of Canada, and Maine in the US seem to respond to the method, and a whole range of flies has been designed for it. Suffice it to say that experimentation is called for, but it is unlikely to take place on the exclusive, best, and therefore expensive rivers of the northern UK.

Salmon may take the dry fly on a dead drift over them, or stripped to make a wake. It can be particularly effective on low rivers with stale fish, and another way is worth consideration that may score as well: some anglers have managed to tempt 'doggo' salmon to the unlikely lure of a well-cast nymph, fished with an induced-take lift.

In the light of this, it is interesting to recall that anglers who have fished for fish-farm salmon stocked into stillwaters, have taken them on all of the flies that they normally use for trout, including tiny dry flies and nymphs. When spooned or gutted, these most stale of stale fish have often had food in their stomachs, possibly grabbed out of the fish-farm feeding reflex, or out of a genuine hunger revived after some time in stillwater.

ABOVE *This specimen rainbow was not going back into the small lake it came from, so after it was cleanly killed it was unhooked for the camera.*

HOOKING SALMON If you strike an Atlantic salmon the instant that you feel a pull, you will occasionally hook one – you may even hook a lot. Opinion is divided as to how to hook the king of game fish, but the majority come down on the side of not striking instantly.

Instead, unlike almost any other fish that takes a fly, let the salmon not just turn down with your fly, but swim away and take line from the reel before you lift the rod and set the hook.

In practice, this means that you hold a loose loop of line between the butt ring and the reel, let the fly swing around on the stream, and when you feel a pull, release the line, letting the fish turn down and away until the reel gives a little 'zizz'. Then you clamp down and lift to set the hook. It is extraordinary how the salmon does hold the fly in the mouth for that long – but it will.

ABOVE Playing a trout on the River Soca, Yugoslavia. Eastern European waters have survived better than those in the west – Yugoslavia has superb 'chalk streams'.

PLAYING A FISH

Having set the hook in your fish's mouth – any fish that is, not just a salmon – you will meet with a number of reactions. Some fish will immediately set off on a long run, salmon, for instance, or large brown trout. Others will instantly leap: tarpon, steelhead, and very often rainbows, sometimes Northern pike. Only experience will prepare you for the options, but there are a number of standard precautions you should take:

● Get the rod up to act as a cushion to the pulls of the fish.

● Do not try to set your brake or drag mechanism, but have it pre-adjusted both to the tackle you are using and to the likely power and weight of the fish sought.

● Unless you are experienced, use adequate tackle. Light-tackle fly fishing is great fun when you can handle the fish, but leaving a fly in a game fish is not sporting, and no fun for the novice. Adequate tackle is a sufficiently powerful rod, a strong enough leader and plenty of backing.

● Plan your likely course of action before you hook a fish. If the place where you are fishing means that you will have to climb a fence and slide down a waterfall to follow a big fish, try to work out an alternative. Of course, if you can only fish it from there, it is a chance you must take.

● Have an adequate net handy if you are going to land your fish and do not intend to release it.

● Do not panic, do not pull too hard, and do not be too gentle, which is the more common fault with novice anglers. It is easier said than done! With most fly rods you could not pull hard enough to break a 5lb (2.2kg) leader – so use the rod, and trust your knots.

● You will often hear the advice to lower the rod when a fish jumps so that your leader does not snap, but to the author slack line in playing a fish is anathema, it is far better to keep a steady tension on the fish. That way it cannot fall on your leader, slack or not, and the hook is kept firmly in place.

● Finally, and perhaps it should have been point seven, enjoy playing your fish. The action you get is not the be-all and end-all of the pleasure of the sport but it is the most important part. So try to relax and admire your opponent in action.

LANDING A TROUT

Net your fish by lowering an adequately sized landing net into the water, drawing the fish over it, and lifting smoothly. Easier said than done? Not really, the only things not allowed for are the minor adjustments (it is easier to move the net 2ft [0.6m] to the left than to try to move the fish). Not for the novice to try are the skills of more advanced anglers or guides who can tease a fish into a net, and who can often scoop a passing fish quickly into the mesh and onto the bank.

Ideally, especially on unstocked rivers and lakes, anglers should be putting a lot of fish back. The time will not be long before even the most hardened Atlantic salmon angler will return the majority of his extinction-threatened catch.

So how do we set about doing this to preserve the species? First, whenever we intend to return fish we should use barbless hooks. There are various types available,

ABOVE A typical Kennet trout comes to net below a manmade fish holding feature – a sluice, or weir.

OPPOSITE Spooning trout is essential to good nymphing – even this small stocked rainbow has a useful lesson to tell in its stomach contents.

and probably Roman Moser's Arrow Points are the best compromise between barbed and barbless. These hooks make the quick return of a fish very easy. Play the fish out, but try not to overdo the pressure and over-stress the fish. Then hold the fly and let the fish wriggle off. A big, exhausted fish may need holding with its nose into the current to revive it as oxygenated water passes over the gills. In stillwater you can gently and slowly swish the fish back and forth so that water flows over its gills.

My favourite method when intending to release a fish hooked on a barbed hook, is to get it into shallow water, tuck the rod under my arm, grasp the leader and hold it tight, then grip the fly in a pair of artery forceps and twitch it out as the fish wriggles. This is less clumsy than using the fingers and less likely to do harm to the fish's mouth or your fingers. A fish that is to be returned should never be netted but if it is, leave the net in the water while unhooking it.

All operations involving handling live fish should be made with wet hands. If caught without a net, it is usually a simple matter to beach a fish. Play it out in the normal way, lead it to a shallow area, where it will roll onto its side, and smoothly draw it up the bank, which must be gently shelving. The flapping of the fish's tail tends to push it farther up the bank, since that is its swimming motion.

A salmon has a tail 'designed' for handling. It is either caught in a lasso-like noose of wire on a stout pole, which is passed over the tail; or the fish is grasped by the 'wrist'

with the thumb and finger towards the tail, which should afford a firm grip. Not for the novice.

CARE OF THE CATCH

It is most unusual to deep-hook a fish on fly tackle, but if you have and it has bled, do not return it. And obviously, if you cannot revive a fish sufficiently for it to swim away, then it is proper to kill it. This should be done with the priest that you should always carry. A firm blow on the head just behind the eyes is the most humane way

to do it. For freshness you may want to retain your catch alive on a stringer. Alternatively you can gut the fish as soon after capture and killing it as possible, and if no cool box or bag is available, keep the fish well wrapped in damp grass or suitable bankside vegetation.

NEVER keep a fish in a plastic bag if you intend to eat it, the old traditional wicker creel, or woven rush bag were ideal containers for fish when these were kept damp, as they cooled by evaporation.

FLY DRESSING

*I*f an angler wants to become a top-class fly fisherman, he must learn the basics of fly dressing. Apart from the sheer enjoyment of tying your own flies, and the ultimate delight of catching a fish on a pattern of your own making, the art of fly tying also enables you to closely match a local hatch, and to copy the successful flies of your friends. Few tools are needed initially, and the basic techniques are really not too hard to learn. Here is a brief look at what you need, and some of the basic techniques.

TOOLS

There are many talented fly dressers who use a few, even no tools, to tie delightful flies, but the novice is well-advised to acquire a small selection. Buy a middle-price range vice, preferable one that will accept a variety of jaws. Do not be tempted by one carrying the many special features that are available — instead go for a basic vice that is easily clamped on a suitable board or table, and with jaws that are easily tightened onto a hook. Also buy a bobbin holder, to hold your fly-tying thread, and make its use easier.

A sharp pointed pair of small scissors is essential to most tyers. Thread and soft items are cut with the tips; harder items like tinsel deep in the jaws, so as not to blunt the tips.

Finally make or buy a bodkin — a sharp point on a handle. This has multiple uses: applying varnish, picking out trapped hackling, fluffing up dubbing, clearing varnish from the hook eye, and separating individual feather fibres. There are innumerable other items that can be bought or made, and may be found useful by the more experienced tyer, but those described here will do to begin with.

THE WHIP FINISH

The novice may not immediately feel the need to learn this universal fly-finishing technique and when he does he can buy a whip finish to help him. At first, a couple of simple half-hitches and a good soaking of varnish will do to finish the flies. But, with a well-waxed fly-tying thread, a simple whip finish obviates the need for varnish altogether. Even varnished half-hitches have a nasty habit of coming undone when the fly has taken

Posed for the camera, this fly dresser has his materials arrayed around him in a disorderly jumble — but in his vice is a beautiful, fully dressed Durham Ranger salmon fly.

FLY DRESSING TOOLS

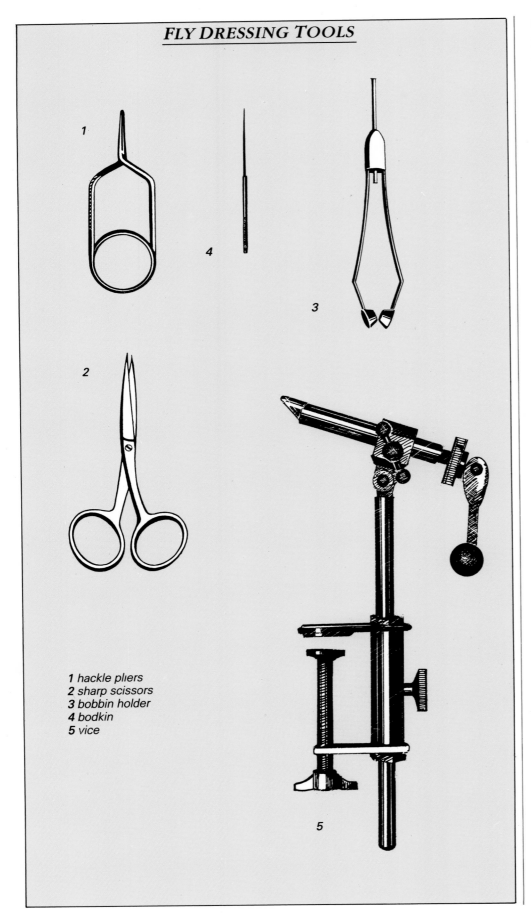

1 hackle pliers
2 sharp scissors
3 bobbin holder
4 bodkin
5 vice

several fish. Practise the whip finish on a needle. If you mess it up, you can slide it off and start again. Start the thread onto the needle as shown in diagrams 1, 2, and 3 of the Imaginary Muddler series.

If you're right-handed, transfer the bobbin holder to the left hand. Take a loop of tying thread around the first two fingers of the left hand as shown. Now take the loop round in three or four turns of thread over the thread from the bobbin holder. Hold the loop open and begin to ease the thread tight, and as the loop tightens, insert the points of your scissors, or a bobbin, to hold it taut as you ease it tight, and you have a whip finish without a whip finish tool the way many professionals do it.

THREE 'FANTASY' FLIES

Here are three purely invented flies that demonstrate a range of basic fly tying techniques. There are dozens more, but these will suffice to begin with.

THE IMAGINARY MUDDLER Having mastered the basic whip finish, starting the thread onto the hook (1, 2, 3) should give you no problems. Wind the thread firmly, without taking it to the verge of snapping, a few turns up the hook shank, then back over itself.

MARIBOU WINGS OR TAILS: Pull off a bunch of maribou, damp the ends and then twist them (4) into a little shuttlecock. This makes them easy to manoeuvre. As you are using this maribou as a tail, tie it in along the hook shank (5) to form an even underbody. All materials are better tied in this way.

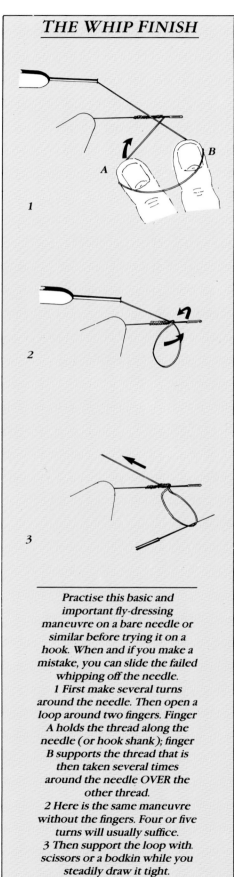

1

2

3

ABOVE Rod up and using the full through-action of his glass rod to combat the pull of a good fish in the heavy current, this Kennet angler is in command.

MYLAR BODIES: Measure the mylar against the hookshank, and cut it neatly. Slip the central core out (6). It pays to make an even underbody to support the mylar. In this case the marabou is thick enough by itself – otherwise build-up with tying thread or perhaps a wind of wool. Wind the thread down to the hook bend, slide the mylar along the shank, and tie it on with several firm wraps of thread. Neatly trim the loose ends of mylar. Varnish the whippings, and cut off the excess thread. Ease the mylar gently but firmly up to the hook eye and tie in by starting the thread again. Clip off the loose ends, and wind over them (7).

HAIR WINGS: The wing illustrated is squirrel hair, but the same rules can be applied to bucktail or synthetic materials. A useful extra tool is a hair stacker. A plastic bottle top suffices (8). Cut the hair from the tail, and drop it tips first into the stacker. This should even up the ends. Grip them firmly between finger and thumb to keep them level, and hold them over the hook shank in a pinch. Tie them in at the head, and trim the hairs at an angle, to produce a tapered head (9).

Practise this basic and important fly-dressing maneuvre on a bare needle or similar before trying it on a hook. When and if you make a mistake, you can slide the failed whipping off the needle.
1 First make several turns around the needle. Then open a loop around two fingers. Finger A holds the thread along the needle (or hook shank); finger B supports the thread that is then taken several times around the needle OVER the other thread.
2 Here is the same maneuvre without the fingers. Four or five turns will usually suffice.
3 Then support the loop with scissors or a bodkin while you steadily draw it tight.

THE IMAGINARY MUDDLER

This imaginary fly teaches starting the thread, the use of marabou, mylar bodies, hair winging, and muddler heads. Always mask the hook point in the vice – the whole hook is shown in the diagrams to let the novice orientate himself.

1 Start the thread this way. Hold the loose end and take a turn over the hook shank.

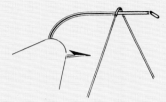

2 Make several turns around the hook shank towards the eye.

4 When working with marabou pull off a large bunch from the centre of the quill. To keep it under control, dampen the quill ends, and twist them together.

5 As you are using the marabou as a tail in this case, pinch it between left finger and thumb and hold it over the hook shank about two-thirds of the way along the shank. Wind the thread down over it to form a smooth underbody.

6 Cut a length of mylar just ½in (12mm) longer than the hook shank. From the centre of the mylar, slip out the core material.

8 Cut a bunch of squirrel tail around one-and-a-half times the hook shank in length. Place this, fine tips down, in a hair stacker – an old bottle top will do.

9 Tie this in on top of the hook shank, pinching it between finger and thumb throughout. After taking several firm turns around the hair cut away the surplus at an angle.

10 Still pinching the wing in place, wind back over it to make a firm base for a muddler head.

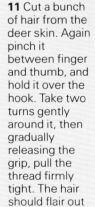

11 Cut a bunch of hair from the deer skin. Again pinch it between finger and thumb, and hold it over the hook. Take two turns gently around it, then gradually releasing the grip, pull the thread firmly tight. The hair should flair out and around the hook at the same time.

12 Compress the hair back towards the wing with the right finger and thumb, and apply another bunch. An extra-efficient method is to use an empty ball point pen case to squeeze the hair. The end result is a little ragged ball of hair. Leave space to finish the fly at the eye of the hook.

13 Trim the hair down to size.

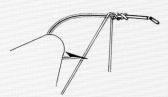

3 Now wind the thread back over itself. If all has been done firmly enough you should be able to clip away the loose end and let the thread hang without slipping.

7 Half hitch the thread at the hook eye and cut it off. Slide the mylar over the underbody, and take several turns of thread over the frayed butts of the mylar. Cover them with several turns of silk, and with the tips of your scissors clip off the surplus ends. Cover them neatly and take several half hitches before dabbing a drop of quick drying varnish on them. Cut away the surplus thread. Now ease the mylar tight along the hook shank with the left hand and make several turns of thread around it just before the hook eye. Clip off the loose fibres and overwhip the ends. Do not make half hitches or cut the thread.

14 The end result shows the head clipped to a bullet shape with a ruff for extra action.

15 Here are other effective muddler head shapes.

MUDDLER HEADS: A firm base will help you to tie a good muddler head. So on this pattern, several firm winds of thread are wound up-and-down over the other materials (10). Cut a bunch of deer-hair, and pinch over the hook shank. Take two loose but firm turns around the hair (11), and ease them tight. This causes the hair to flare out (12). In this case the fine tips of the hair have been left pointing to the rear as part of the wing or rudimentary 'gills'. Repeat the process (13), compressing each bunch of hair towards the hook bend between finger and thumb. The result is a raggy, shaving brush effect, which needs trimming to shape (14), with a sharp pair of scissors, or even a razor blade. A wide variety of head shapes is possible (15). Whip finish and varnish.

THE NEVER-NEVER NYMPH This invented nymph is a decent damsel or dragonfly nymph pattern, but it teaches other techniques. Start the thread as before, and begin the fly by tying the wire rib and a tail of cock pheasant tail fibres along the hook shank, again, to make an even body.

CHENILLE BODIES: Strip the fluff from the core of a length of chenille over the last quarter inch (1). Tie it in by the stripped core to reduce bulk (2). Wind it evenly up the hook shank leaving space for a thorax (3). Trim the excess chenille.

BELOW Roll casting to salmon on Scotland's River Lyon.

ABOVE *A trout succumbs to a tempting fly in shallow Norwegian waters.*

PALMERED HACKLES: Exactly the same technique will be used for tying all hackles, but palmered hackles are wound along the hook shank, instead of one or more turns. Prepare the hackles (4) by stripping off the base fluff and fibres. Tie the fly in at right angles to the hook shank, and wind the hackle in open even turns back to the hook bend (6) (hackle pliers can be a useful tool to grip the hackle, but are not essential). Trap the hackle in place by winding the wire rib through the opposite spiral through the hackle in open turns. Tie it off and clip off the hackle tip, and the excess wire rib.

WINGCASES AND SHELLBACKS: The same basic technique can be applied to both wingcases and shellbacks. Pull a bunch of cock pheasant (or other feather) fibres from the quill, and tie them in, in a bunch on top of the hook shank tips pointing out past the bend (9). They should equal the tail length to work best when used as legs later.

DUBBING: The basic technique to provide fur bodies. A synthetic dubbing is used in this example. It can help to wax the thread (7). Pinch out a small bunch of dubbing, and pull out the fibres into fine separate fibres. Squeeze them onto the thread between finger and thumb (8), and twist them onto the thread in one direction only. The result should be a neat slim sausage of dubbing with the thread at the core (9). The thorax should be a neat round or oval blob, when wound (10).

LEGS: A useful way of producing basic legs is to pull the wingcase fibres over the thorax, and tie them in at the head. Divide them with the silk, fold them back under the thorax, and form a neat head. Feather fibre tips should just touch the hook point. Whip-finish and varnish.

THE WONDERLAND WET FLY TIPPET TAILS: The tail of this fly is made of golden pheasant tippets, which are an excellent material to practise the correct alignment of the tips with, as each tip consists of a dark blob — further down the

THE NEVER-NEVER NYMPH

This teaches the use of chenille, fibre tails, preparation and palmering of hackles, ribbing, and dubbing.

1 Prepare a 4in (10cm) length of olive green chenille. To do this strip away the fluff from the core over ¼in (6mm).

2 Place a long-shank hook in the vice. For ease of illustration most of the hook is shown — you should mask the point and barb inside the jaws of the vice. Start the thread a little behind the eye and run it down the hook and back up in neat touching turns. Now clip seven or eight pheasant tail fibres off the quill, and pinch them between the finger and thumb of your left hand, and hold them over the hook shank. Tie them in on top of the hook shank and take several turns over them to support them — tie in a four inch length of silver wire or tinsel, at the same time. Taking the thread over both materials wind it down to the bend, and tie in the core of chenille — this gives a smooth bump-free underbody.

3 Take the thread two-thirds of the way back up the hook shank, and leave it to hang. Now wind the chenille up to the same position and tie it in. Clip off the excess chenille.

4 Prepare a dyed olive hen hackle by pulling all the fluff from the bottom of the quill.

5 Tie this hackle in beside the chenille as shown. The length of the fibres should roughly equal the gape of the hook.

6 Wind the hackle down to the bend in open turns. Take the wire back through it in the opposite spiral to lock it in place. Tie it off, and cut off the hackle tip and the surplus wire.

7 If you find dubbing difficult, wax the thread (if you are using unwaxed tying thread).

8 Dub the thread by twisting the dubbing IN ONE DIRECTION ONLY. Spread it along the thread as you go — for about 1in (2.5cm) of thread. Now ease it down the thread a little.

9 Take about a dozen cock pheasant fibres, pinch them together and tie them in on top of the hook shank. Now wind on the dubbing to make a neat oval-shaped thorax.

10 Complete the fly by pulling over the cock pheasant tails to make a wing case. Divide the tips of the fibres in two halves and draw them back to lie along the thorax as 'legs'. Whip finish the head and varnish.

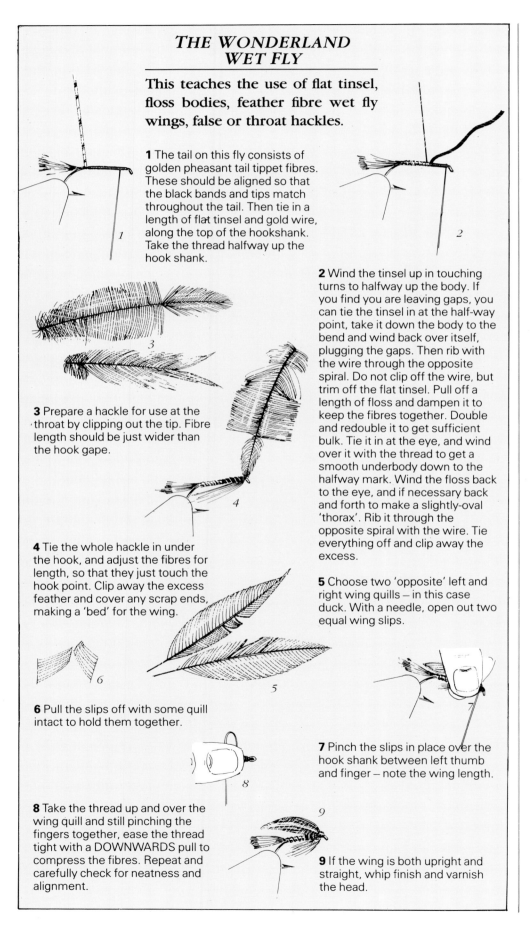

THE WONDERLAND WET FLY

This teaches the use of flat tinsel, floss bodies, feather fibre wet fly wings, false or throat hackles.

1 The tail on this fly consists of golden pheasant tail tippet fibres. These should be aligned so that the black bands and tips match throughout the tail. Then tie in a length of flat tinsel and gold wire, along the top of the hookshank. Take the thread halfway up the hook shank.

3 Prepare a hackle for use at the throat by clipping out the tip. Fibre length should be just wider than the hook gape.

4 Tie the whole hackle in under the hook, and adjust the fibres for length, so that they just touch the hook point. Clip away the excess feather and cover any scrap ends, making a 'bed' for the wing.

6 Pull the slips off with some quill intact to hold them together.

8 Take the thread up and over the wing quill and still pinching the fingers together, ease the thread tight with a DOWNWARDS pull to compress the fibres. Repeat and carefully check for neatness and alignment.

2 Wind the tinsel up in touching turns to halfway up the body. If you find you are leaving gaps, you can tie the tinsel in at the half-way point, take it down the body to the bend and wind back over itself, plugging the gaps. Then rib with the wire through the opposite spiral. Do not clip off the wire, but trim off the flat tinsel. Pull off a length of floss and dampen it to keep the fibres together. Double and redouble it to get sufficient bulk. Tie it in at the eye, and wind over it with the thread to get a smooth underbody down to the halfway mark. Wind the floss back to the eye, and if necessary back and forth to make a slightly-oval 'thorax'. Rib it through the opposite spiral with the wire. Tie everything off and clip away the excess.

5 Choose two 'opposite' left and right wing quills – in this case duck. With a needle, open out two equal wing slips.

7 Pinch the slips in place over the hook shank between left thumb and finger – note the wing length.

9 If the wing is both upright and straight, whip finish and varnish the head.

feather is another black stripe. Tie them in along the hookshank.

TINSEL BODIES: Next tie in the gold wire ribbing, again along the shank. There is no need to cut the flat tinsel at an angle. Tie it straight along the hook, too (1). Wind the tinsel in flat touching turns halfway down the hook. When tying a whole body, tie the tinsel in at the eye, then wind it down to the bend, and back again, covering any gaps. These usually stem from an uneven underbody.

WIRE RIBS: Rib with the wire through the opposite spiral. Tie off the rib at the end of the tinsel, but do not cut off the excess wire (2).

FLOSS BODIES: Some floss needs doubling to make it quicker and easier to build up a body. Dampen the floss with saliva to lessen the chance of fraying. Wind a slightly oval front section of the body, and rib with gold wire, tying it in at the head and cutting away the excess (4).

FALSE HACKLES: Where a false or throat hackle is required, the simplest system is to take a whole hackle, and clip the tip out of it (3). Tie the remainder in under the hook, adjusting the tips for length before clipping off the rest of the hackle, which after trimming can be used again. False hackles should just touch the hook point (4).

FEATHER FIBRE WINGS: A few winds of thread now make a firm base for the feather fibre wing, which is prepared as shown. Two matched feathers should be used – in this case a pair of bleached and dyed cinnamon duck wing quills (5). An equal slip of feather fibres is separated on each feather, and detached if possible by pulling off so that a strip of quill adheres to the fibres and holds them together (6). Otherwise cut the slips and manipulate them with your bodkin. The matched feathers come from each wing, and mirror-image each other – the slips will generally be taken from the wide side. They, too, will mirror each other (6). Pinch the slips between finger and thumb of the left hand, and measure them up over the hook shank (7). Now change the grip (8), to hold the slips paired and flat over the hook, and take the thread over them between the pinched fingers and back down again. Ease the thread tight slowly downwards to compress the fibres. The result should be two upright perfectly-matched wing slips. Their length should just equal the length of the tail fibres (9).

The preceding techniques enable the tying of thousands of killing patterns. Refer to the bibliography for some real masterpieces of fly-dressing techniques.

RIGHT In action on the Frying Pan River, Colorado, where catch and release is compulsory.

POPULAR FLY PATTERNS

A number of factors influence the styles and dressings of modern flies. Many more traditional fly dressers would like to preserve the original dressings of the old patterns intact, with few changes to rare and noble 'breeds'. Now this is frequently impossible, as the old days when rare fur and feather were cobbled together to form a deadly salmon fly have passed. Today we must be more conservationist in our approach. Take the simple case of seal fur, a popular material in the UK particularly and vital to classics like the Mallard and Claret; legislation now states that synthetic materials be used for dubbing. Is there a loss of quality or effectiveness? There are a few superstitious – or more sensitive – anglers who believe their fly materials must be 'natural' to appeal to the fish. However, there is very little of the 'natural' remaining in thoroughly cleansed, dyed and chopped seal fur. In practice, synthetic materials can attract fish just as readily.

Colour may be of more significance. Generally it is advisable to avoid dyeing materials a specific colour; instead blend several different shades together. Close examination of most insects shows that they have a widely varying range of colours in their make up. Terms such as grey midge are very deceptive. Grey, red, yellow, amber and green might better describe the midge's stippled shades as revealed under magnification.

Flashy materials are now common and, as with a dash of fluorescent material, a few strands have a deadly role to play in prey-fish and hatching-nymph patterns.

Good fly fishing is a combination of presentation, accuracy of cast, followed by the right retrieve – and the right fly. However, it is often the case of 'not what you fish, but the way you fish it'. So do not be afraid to fish your less-than-perfect flies with complete confidence – fish only award a very few points for tidiness! In the meantime put in plenty of practice, concentrating on durability – that is tightness of dressing with the minimum use of silk.

Here are the recipes for some great international flies. But remember that they represent only a fraction of available patterns and slight changes in the dressing or material could as easily improve the original as ruin it.

ROYAL WULFF

Dry Fly

HOOK: 10 to 14 downeye.
THREAD: Black
WING: White calf tail, upright and divided.
TAIL: Natural deer body hair.
BODY: Two sections of peacock herl divided by red floss.
HACKLE: Natural brown cock.

YELLOW HUMPY

Dry Fly

HOOK: 10 to 14 downeye.
THREAD: Yellow
TAIL: Natural deer hair tips.
UNDERBODY: Yellow floss or polypropylene.
BODY: Deer hair.
WING: Tips of deer hair body.
HACKLE: Grizzle cock.

IRRESISTIBLE

Dry Fly

HOOK: 10 to 14 (larger for salmon).
TAIL: Black-dyed deer hair tips.
BODY: Natural deer hair spun muddler-style.
WINGS: Grizzle hackle tips.
HACKLE: Natural red cock and grizzle mixed.

ADAMS

Dry Fly

HOOK: 10 to 20 downeye.
THREAD: Grey
TAIL: Mixed grizzle and natural red hackle fibres.
BODY: Grey poly dubbing.
WING: Grizzle hackle tips.
HACKLE: Natural red cock and grizzle mixed.

BLACK GNAT

Dry Fly

HOOK: 8 to 20 downeye.
THREAD: Black
TAIL: Black cock hackle fibres.
BODY: Black dyed mole or poly dubbing.
WING: Grey mallard slips.
HACKLE: Black cock.

MOSQUITO

Dry Fly

HOOK: 12 to 20 downeye.
THREAD: Black
TAIL: Grizzle hackle fibres.
BODY: Striped grizzle cock hackle; or black floss ribbed with grizzle cock hackle.
WING: Grizzle cock.
HACKLE: Grizzle cock.

MARCH BROWN

Dry Fly

HOOK: 12 to 16 downeye.
THREAD: Yellow
WING: Wood duck upright and divided.
TAIL: Brown hackle fibres.
BODY: Fawn hare's ear or poly dubbing.
HACKLE: Brown and grizzle mixed.

BROWN BIVISIBLE

Dry Fly

HOOK: 10 to 14 downeye.
THREAD: Black
TAIL: Brown hackle fibres.
BODY: Three natural brown cock hackles palmered in increasing size to just before the eye.
HACKLE: Three turns natural white or cream cock hackle.

PALE OLIVE SPINNER

Dry Fly

HOOK: 14 to 20 downeye.
THREAD: Olive
WING: Olive grey polywing/white hackle fibres, tied spent-style.
TAIL: Light dun hackle fibres.
BODY: Pale olive seal's fur or poly substitute.

BLACK ANT

Dry Fly

HOOK: 14 to 24 downeye.
THREAD: Black micro
BODY: Two separate balls of dubbing, seal's fur or poly substitute.
HACKLE: In centre of body, sparse black hackle.

BEETLE

Dry Fly

HOOK: 14 to 20 downeye.
THREAD: Black
SHELLBACK: Grey goose fibre (also dyed black or brown).
BODY: Peacock herl/black ostrich.
HACKLE: Black palmered, then clipped short.

MACMURRAY ANT

Dry Fly

One of an extraordinary and successful series of balsa bodied flies to imitate a host of aquatic and terrestrial insects.
HOOK: 16 to 20 downeye.
THREAD: To match body.
BODY: Two tiny 'blobs' of balsa wood, carved to size, joined with fine monofilament and tied in place at the centre.
HACKLE: Tiny grizzle on this example – natural red to match red ant, black to match black ant.

PHEASANT TAIL DRY

Dry Fly

HOOKS: 14 to 20 upeye.
THREAD: Brown micro
TAIL: Two or three strands of cock pheasant fibres.
BODY: Cock pheasant tail fibre.
RIB: Fine gold wire or better, monofilament of 2lb (1kg) B.S.
HACKLE: Natural red cock.

WICKHAM'S FANCY DRY

Dry Fly

Tied with the wings swept back this is a superb wet fly; also tied without a wing as an excellent palmered fly. Tail fibres can be substituted on palmered version with fluorescent green or red floss.
HOOK: 14 to 18 upeye.
THREAD: Black or brown.
TAIL: Natural red cock hackle fibres.
BODY: Flat gold tinsel.
RIB: Gold wire, also locks hackle in place.
HACKLE: Palmered natural red cock.
WING: Upright slips of grey duck.
COLLAR HACKLE: Natural red cock.

GREENWELL'S GLORY DRY

Dry Fly

HOOK: 12 to 18 upeye.
TAIL: Furnace cock hackle fibres.
BODY: Dark olive thread (traditionally golden olive darkened with dubbing wax).
RIB: Gold wire or tinsel.
WING: Grey duck slips upright.
HACKLE: Furnace cock.

GREY DUSTER

Dry Fly

HOOK: 14 to 18 upeye.
THREAD: Grey
BODY: Grey rabbit underfur or natural mole.
HACKLE: Badger cock.

GREY WULFF MAYFLY

Dry Fly

HOOK: Mayfly longshank upeye, 8 to 12.
TAIL: White tips of grey squirrel tail.
BODY: Grey poly, or natural mole.
WING: Forward-slanted divided bunches of grey squirrel tail white tips.
HACKLE: Large blue/grey dun cock hackle.

RICHARD WALKER CRANE FLY (DADDY OR HARRY LONGLEGS)

Dry Fly

HOOKS: Longshank 6 to 12.
THREAD: Brown
BODY: Cinnamon feather fibres.
WINGS: Ginger hackle points.
HACKLE: Ginger cock.
LEGS: At least eight cock hackle fibres knotted twice to represent joints of the legs.

HAWTHORN

Dry Fly

HOOK: 10 to 12 downeye (upeye in illustration, but see below).
THREAD: Black
BODY: Two thirds black floss.
THORAX: Other third of body, peacock or black dyed ostrich herl.
WING: White hackle tips.
HACKLE: Black cock, or possibly hen, see below.
NB Natural flies sit in, not on surface film, so a downeye hook is probably a better choice to sit the artificial fly in film. Likewise, soft hen may be a better choice than cock.

ELK HAIR CADDIS

Dry Fly

Although this is a dry fly it can also be effective pulled, or even as a waking top dropper for traditional tactics.
HOOK: 8 to 14 downeye.
THREAD: To match body.
BODY: Yellow, green or orange polyarn, or suitable buoyant fibre.
HACKLE: Palmered brown or natural red cock.
WING: Elk hair tied as roof shaped wing, clipped square ends protruding to make wake on water.

INVICTA

Classic Wet Fly

HOOKS: 6 to 16 downeye.
THREAD: Golden olive.
TAIL: Golden pheasant crest.
BODY: Golden olive seal's fur or substitute.
HACKLE: Palmered natural red
THROAT HACKLE: Blue jay black and blue fibres; dyed blue gallena is substitute.
WING: Hen pheasant tail.

MALLARD AND CLARET

Classic Wet Fly

HOOK: 10 to 16 downeye.
THREAD: Claret or brown.
TAIL: Golden pheasant tippets.
BODY: Claret seal's fur or substitute.
RIB: Golden oval tinsel or wire in smaller sizes.
WING: Bronze mallard slips.
THROAT OR FALSE HACKLE: Claret-dyed hen.

BUTCHER

Classic Wet Fly

HOOK: 6 to 18 downeye.
THREAD: Black
TAIL: Slip of red feather fibre/fluorescent red floss.
BODY: Flat silver tinsel.
RIB: Silver oval tinsel or wire.
WING: Black feather fibre.
THROAT OR FALSE HACKLE: Black hen.

ZULU

Classic Wet Fly

HOOK: 6 to 18 downeye.
THREAD: Black
TAIL: Red wool or fluorescent floss.
BODY: Black dubbed seal's fur or wool.
RIB: Silver oval tinsel or wire.
HACKLE: Palmered black cock or hen.

CONNEMARA BLACK

Classic Wet Fly

HOOK: 6 to 18.
THREAD: Black
TAIL: Golden pheasant crest.
BODY: Black seal's fur or substitute.
RIB: Silver oval tinsel.
WING: Bronze mallard.
HACKLE: Two: black cock or hen, with blue jay over.

DUNKELD

Classic Wet Fly

HOOKS: 6 to 18; longshanks 6 to 10 for sea trout and Atlantic salmon.
THREAD: Brown
TAIL: Golden pheasant crest.
BODY: Flat gold tinsel.
RIB: Fine gold oval tinsel or wire.
WING: Bronze mallard.
HACKLE: Orange-dyed cock or hen false or throat hackle; the fly is often palmered with an orange hackle, too.
EYES OR CHEEKS: Jungle cock or substitute.

RED OR SOLDIER PALMER

Classic Wet Fly

HOOK: 6 to 18 downeye, occasionally longshank 10 to 12.
THREAD: Brown or orange.
TAIL (OPTIONAL): Red fluorescent floss, red wool, natural red hackle fibres.
BODY: Red seal's fur or substitute.
RIB: Gold fine oval tinsel or wire.
HACKLE: Palmered, natural red cock or hen.

TEAL BLUE AND SILVER

Classic Wet Fly

HOOKS: 6 to 16, also longshanks as Dunkeld.
THREAD: Black
TAIL: Golden pheasant tippets.
BODY: Flat silver tinsel.
RIB: Fine oval silver or silver wire.
WING: Silver teal.
HACKLE: False or throat blue dyed cock or hen.
Note Although not recognisably insects, most of the above have achieved success in insect hatches; for midges try the Mallard and Claret, Butcher, Zulu, Connemara Black, Dunkeld, and Red Palmer; for caddis (sedges) try the Invicta, Dunkeld, or Red Palmer; the Butcher, Dunkeld and Teal, Blue, and Silver, make effective small fish imitators.

LIGHT CAHILL

Wet Fly

HOOK: 10 to 14 downeye.
THREAD: Tan or cream.
TAIL: Cream hackle fibres.
BODY: Cream dubbing.
HACKLE: Fully wound cream hen.
WING: Lemon wood duck.

DARK HENDRICKSON

Wet Fly

HOOK: 10 to 14 downeye.
THREAD: Grey
TAIL: Medium dun hackle fibres.
BODY: Muskrat, polydub, or undyed mole.
HACKLE: Medium dun hen, fully wound.
WING: Lemon wood duck.

COACHMAN

Wet Fly

HOOKS: 10 to 16 downeye.
THREAD: Black or dark green.
TAG: Optional gold flat tinsel.
BODY: Peacock herl.
HACKLE: Dark ginger hen, fully wound.
WING: White duck.

MONTANA NYMPH

Nymph

HOOK: Longshank 8 to 14.
THREAD: Black
UNDERBODY: Lead wire optional.
TAIL: Black hackle fibres.
BODY: Black chenille.
WINGCASE: Black chenille.
THORAX: Yellow chenille.
HACKLE: Black cock or hen palmered over thorax.
NB A common British version substitute fluorescent green chenille for yellow thorax to great effect.

TED'S STONEFLY

Nymph

HOOKS: Longshank 8 to 14.
THREAD: Brown
UNDERBODY: Lead wire optional.
TAIL: Two brown dyed goose biots, divided.
BODY: Brown chenille.
WINGCASE: Brown chenille.
THORAX: Orange chenille.
HACKLE: Palmered brown cock or hen over thorax.

ZUG BUG

Nymph

HOOK: 8 to 12 longshank.
THREAD: Black or green.
UNDERBODY: Lead wire optional.
TAIL: Peacock sword fibres.
RIB: Oval silver tinsel.
BODY: Peacock herl.
HACKLE: Brown hen false hackle.
WINGCASE: Lemon woodduck of silver mallard, clipped short.

PRINCE

Nymph

HOOK: 8 to 12 longshank.
UNDERBODY: Lead wire optional.
THREAD: Black or brown.
TAIL: Two brown-dyed goose biots.
BODY: Peacock herl.
RIB: Fine oval gold tinsel.
HACKLE: Two turns brown cock hackle.
HORNS OR WING: Two white goose biots.

TELLICO

Nymph

HOOK: Longshank 10 to 14; standard downeye 8 to 12.
THREAD: Yellow or black
UNDERBODY: Lead wire optional.
TAIL: Guinea fowl hackle fibres.
WINGCASE: Cock pheasant tail fibres.
RIB: Peacock herl.
BODY: Yellow floss.
HACKLE: Brown hen fully wound.
NB To protect the peacock a little, rib through opposite spiral with gold wire.

GOLD RIBBED HARE'S EAR

Nymph

HOOK: 8 to 18 standard or longshank.
THREAD: Brown
UNDERBODY: Lead wire optional.
TAIL: Furnace hackle fibres.
RIB: Gold oval tinsel or wire.
BODY: Well mixed hare's mask fur.
WINGCASE: Cock or hen pheasant tail fibres.
NB Often improved by including plenty of guard hairs and picking out the dressing.

GREY NYMPH

Nymph

HOOK: 8 to 12 standard or longshank.
THREAD: Black or grey.
UNDERBODY: Lead wire optional.
TAIL: Grizzle hackle fibres.
BODY: Muskrat or natural mole fur.
HACKLE: Fully wound grizzle hen.

OLIVE SCUD

Nymph

HOOK: 12 or 14 standard shanks (grub or sedge-shaped hooks imitate the scud [or shrimp] well).
UNDERBODY: Lead wire optional.
BODY: Olive and orange seal's fur, blended with a little hare's ear.
BACK: Clear polythene or olive raffia.
RIB: Over body and back to imitate segmentation.

GREY GOOSE

Nymph

HOOKS: 12 to 16 downeye.
THREAD: None – use fine copper wire.
TAILS, BODY, AND WINGCASE: Grey goose fibres.
RIB: Copper wire.

PHEASANT TAIL NYMPH

Nymph

HOOKS: 12 to 16 downeye.
THREAD: None – use fine copper wire.
TAILS, BODY AND WINGCASE: Cock pheasant tail fibres.
RIB: Copper wire.

BOW TIE BUZZER

Nymph

HOOKS: 12 to 16 downeye.
THREAD: Micro brown.
TAILS: Cock pheasant tail fibre points.
UNDERBODY: Silver tinsel.
BODY: Cock pheasant fibres wound to show silver underbody.
BREATHERS: A tiny piece of white wool. The nylon leader is threaded through the hook eye, then the wool is tied to the end. The fly hangs in the water like a midge.

SHIPMAN'S BUZZER (MIDGE)

Nymph

HOOK: Downeye 8 to 16.
SILK: Brown.
BREATHERS: White baby wool.
BODY: Brown seal's fur or substitute.
RIB: Pearlescent tape.
NB Fished 'flat' in the surface film.

BLOODWORM

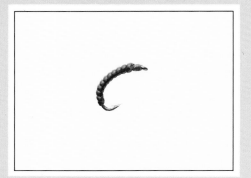

Nymph

HOOK: Sedge-shaped 10 to 16.
SILK: Brown or red.
BODY: Red plastic strip (Swanundaze or similar).

EYEBROOK CADDIS

Nymph

HOOKS: Longshank 12 and 14.
THREAD: Black.
BODY: Dubbed beige-dyed mole.
THORAX: Tiny band of fluorescent green floss.
HACKLE: Very sparse natural black hen.
NB Designed for a famous reservoir.

GLITTER SPIDER

Nymph

HOOKS: Downeye 12 to 16.
THREAD: Black or orange fine.
BODY: Dressed short, irridescent orange glitter material (or other colours).
HACKLE: Sparse orange hen (or other colours).
NB A traditional spider pattern brought lethally up-to-date — use when midges hatch.

FRASER NYMPH

Nymph

HOOKS: Longshank 12 to 16.
THREAD: Beige.
TAILS: Hen pheasant tail fibres.
BODY: Dressed short, irridescent orange glitter material (or other colours).
RIB: Beige cotton.
THORAX: Palest hare's ear.
WINGCASE AND LEGS: As body.
NB Also has green version with green-dyed mole thorax, green cotton rib. Deadly all round nymph.

CARNILL'S ADULT BUZZER (MIDGE)

Nymph

HOOK: Sedge-shaped 10 to 16.
THREAD: Grey.
BODY: Grey goose fibres.
RIB: Stripped peacock herl.
WINGS: Two blue dun hackle tips.
THORAX: Grey natural mole.
HACKLE: Blue dun fibres.
WINGCASE: Grey goose fibres.
NB Fished just under the surface film on the top dropper — not as a dry fly.

BLACK MATUKA OR ACE OF SPADES

Streamer Lure

HOOK: Longshank 6 to 10.
THREAD: Black.
BODY: Black chenille.
RIB: Oval silver tinsel.
WING: Pair of matched black hen hackles.
HACKLE: Fully wound black hen (Ace of Spades: throat hackle of blue jay).
OVERWING (ACE OF SPADES ONLY): Bronze mallard.

MUDDLER MINNOW

Streamer Lure

HOOK: 4 to 12 longshank and standard shanks.
THREAD: Black or brown.
TAIL: Mottled turkey quill or substitute.
BODY: Flat gold tinsel.
UNDERWING: Grey squirrel tail.
OVERWING: Mottled turkey slips or substitute.
HEAD: Spun natural deer hair.

MICKEY FINN

Streamer Lure

HOOK: 4 to 12 longshank.
THREAD: Black or red fluorescent tying thread.
BODY: Silver mylar.
TAG: Butt of red thread to cover end of mylar.
WING: Yellow bucktail, red, then yellow bucktail.

BLACK GHOST

Streamer Lure

HOOK: Longshank 6 to 10.
THREAD: Black.
TAIL: Yellow hackle fibres.
BODY: Tying thread or black floss.
RIB: Silver oval tinsel.
HACKLE: Yellow throat of hackle fibres.
WING: Two or more matched white cock hackles.

WOOLY BUGGER

Streamer Lure

HOOKS: Longshank 6 to 14.
THREAD: Black or to match body.
TAIL: Black marabou (or other colours).
BODY: Black seal's fur or substitute.
HACKLE: Palmered black (or to match body).
RIB: Optional, monofilament.
NB Could be tied in a wide range of colours, and can be leaded at the head, along the body, or unleaded. Bestrides the boundary between nymph and lure.

GARRY DOG

Atlantic Salmon Tube Fly

HOOK: None, tied on tube of plastic or metal in various lengths.
THREAD: Black.
BODY: Black floss.
RIB: Silver oval tinsel.
WING: Two halves, red and yellow bucktail.

HAIRY MARY

Atlantic Salmon Tube Fly

HOOK: None, tied on tube of plastic or metal in various lengths.
THREAD: Black.
BODY: Black floss.
RIB: Silver oval tinsel.
WING: Four, natural bucktail and dyed blue bucktail on each side.

HAIRWING BLUE CHARM

Standard Salmon Fly

HOOKS: 2 to 12, single, double and treble salmon hooks.
THREAD: Black.
TAIL: Golden pheasant crest.
BUTT: Two turns gold tinsel and yellow floss.
BODY: Black floss.
RIB: Gold tinsel.
WING: Natural brown squirrel.
HACKLE: Blue-dyed hackle fibre throat.

BLACK BEAR – GREEN BUTT

Standard Salmon Fly

HOOKS: 2 to 12, single, double and treble salmon hooks.
THREAD: Black.
TAIL: Black bear hair or black cock hackle fibres.
BUTT: Fluorescent green floss.
BODY: Embossed gold tinsel or equivalent.
RIB: Gold tinsel.
WING: Black bear or black dyed squirrel.
HACKLE: Black-dyed cock throat.

BUCK BUG

Pacific Salmon Fly

HOOKS: Low water salmon 2 to 8.
THREAD: Grey or brown.
TAIL: Brown bucktail.
BUTT: Yellow fluorescent floss.
BODY: Natural deer hair.
HACKLE: Palmered brown cock, heavy at shoulder.

GLASS MINNOW

Saltwater Fly

Again a useful prey fish imitator, correctly coloured, anywhere.
HOOKS: 2 to 10 longshank.
THREAD: Olive.
TAIL: Tuft of olive marabou.
BODY: Silver or pearl mylar tubing, the back painted or penned olive.
HEAD: Olive with painted eye.

WHITE DECEIVER

Saltwater Fly

An excellent prey fish imitator anywhere, also tied in red/white, blue/white, and red/yellow versions.
HOOKS: 2/0 to 4; smaller for freshwater use.
THREAD: White or black.
BODY: Silver mylar tubing extended beyond hook bend, and frayed into long strands.
WINGS: Two, long white bucktail above and below the hook shank.
TAILS: Four white cock hackles.
HEAD: Black varnish with white eye.

SELECT BIBLIOGRAPHY

FISHING TECHNIQUES

GRAESSER, Neil, *Advanced Salmon Fishing*, Boydell & Brewer Ltd., Woodbridge, Suffolk, England, 1987

MERWIN, John, (Ed.), *Stillwater Trout*, Nick Lyons Books, Doubleday & Co. Inc., New York, 1980

ENTOMOLOGY

WHITLOCK, Dave, *Guide to Aquatic Trout Foods*, Nick Lyons/ Winchester Press Book, Benn Bros., New York, 1982

SPECIALIST FISHING TECHNIQUES

FRASER, Gordon, *Mastering the Nymph*, Blandford Press, Stirling Publishing Co. Inc., New York; Capricorn Link (Australia) Pty Ltd., Lane Cove, NSW; 1987

PARTON, Steve, *Boatfishing for Trout*, Allen & Unwin Ltd., London; Allen & Unwin Inc., Winchester, Mass.; Allen & Unwin (Australia) Pty Ltd., North Sydney, NSW; 1983

LOCH, LOUGH, AND ATLANTIC SALMON AND SEA TROUT FISHING

CURRIE, Bill, *Days and Nights of Game Fishing*, Allen & Unwin Ltd., London; Allen & Unwin (Australia) Pty Ltd., North Sydney, NSW; Allen & Unwin (New Zealand) Ltd., with Port Nicholson Press, Wellington; 1984

KINGSMILL MOORE, T. C., *A Man May Fish*, Colin Smythe Ltd., Gerrards Cross, Bucks., England; Colin Smythe-Humanities Press Inc., Atlantic Highlands, NJ; 1979

FLY DRESSING AND FLIES

HELLEKSON, Terry, *Popular Fly Patterns*, Gibbs M. Smith Inc., Peregrine Smith Books, Salt Lake City, UT, 1984

LIVELY, Chauncy, *Chauncy Lively's Flybox: A Portfolio of Modern Trout Flies*, Stackpole Books, Harrisburg, PA; Thomas Nelson & Sons Ltd., Ontario, Canada; 1980

MARTIN, Darrel, *Fly-Tying Methods*, David & Charles, Newton Abbot, Devon, England, 1987

PRICE, Taff, *Fly Patterns: An International Guide*, Ward Lock Ltd., London, 1987

WULFF, Lee, *Lee Wulff on Flies*, Stackpole Books, Harrisburg, PA; Thomas Nelson & Sons, Ontario, Canada; 1980

INDEX

Page numbers in italics indicate the sites of relevant captions

A

Adams 110
American brook trout *see* brook trout
arctic grayling 31
Atlantic salmon *28, 29, 36, 70,* 91

B

Baby Doll 56
back casting 24, 25
backing 12, 18–20, 45
 hollow 18
barrier creams 15
bass
 largemouth 32, *35*
 smallmouth 32, *35*
Bass Bug 91
Battisti, Vinnie *50*
Beetle 112
belt pack systems 14
Black Ant 112
Black Bear – Green Butt 124
Black Ghost 122
Black Gnat 111
Black Matuka 122
Black Spider 89
blind fishing 85, 87
blood knot 22, *22*
Bloodworm 120
blood-worms 65–67
blueback *see* sockeye salmon
blue damselflies *64*
bluegill sunfish 32
bonefish 35, *35*
Booby *90,* 91
Bow Tie Buzzer 120
braking 12
brook trout (charr) *28, 29, 36,* 49
Brown Bivisible 111
brown trout 26, *28, 36,* 49, *88*
Buck Bug 124
buoyant fly/sunk line technique 91
Butcher 115
buzzers *see* midges

C

caddis flies (sedge flies) *60,* 61–62, *61, 69,* 89
Carnill's Adult Buzzer (Midge) 121
Carra, Lough 26
cast connectors 20
casting 8, 18, 22–25, *59,* 75, 82
 back 24, *25*
 double-haul 10, 24
 front 24
 length of 10, 11
 loop and 24–25
 overhead 22–23, 24, *24, 25*
 over-the-front (loch) *76*
 roll *18,* 22, 25, *103*
 shortlining 77
 side 11, 24, *25, 76,* 77–78
 single-haul 23–24
 steeple 25
 wind and 25
charr *see* brook trout
chinook *see* Pacific salmon
clippers 14, *14*
clothing 15, *15*

Coachman 117
coho salmon *see* silver salmon
Conn, Lough 49
Connemara Black 116
Corrib, Lough 49
Cove (water) knot 21–22, *22*
crab 57
craneflies (daddy-longlegs, harry-longlegs) 65, 67–68, *67*
crayfish (yabby) *56,* 57
crustacea 57
 see also individual crustacean names
cut-throat trout 26, *28*
cyanoacrilate glue 16, 18–20

D

daddy-longlegs *see* craneflies
damselflies 62–65, *63, 64*
dapping 90–91, *91*
dapping flies *90*
Dark Hendrickson 117
dayflies *see* mayflies
diptera 65–68
dog (chum) salmon 31
Dolly Varden 29
double-haul casting 10, 24
double-taper lines 10–11
dragonflies 62–65, *63, 64*
drogues *76,* 77
droppers 13, 88
 top *77, 77*
dubbing 104, 108
Dunkeld 116
Durham Ranger *98*

E

Eagle River *28, 80*
Elk Hair Caddis 114
emergency nail knot *21*
Ennell, Lough *91*
Esk, River *50, 83*
Eye Brook 48
Eyebrook Caddis 121

F

Falkus, Hugh *83*
ferox trout 49
fish types 26–35
 sea 35
flies 13–14, 16–17, 49, 54–71, *90,* 91–92, 110–24
 care of 16
 dressing 98–107, *98, 108*
 materials for 108
 tools for 98, *100*
 dry 14, 69–70, *69,* 72, 80–83, 89, 91, 110–14
 eggs 56
 leaded point 87–88
 palmered 70–71, *70, 77,* 104
 patterns of, *90,* 108–24
 salmon 123–24, *54, 70, 70, 71, 71*
 saltwater 124
 tube *70, 71, 91,* 123
 tying 13
 wet 14, 70–71, 72–80, 115–117
 winged wet *70*
 see also
 midges
 nymphs
 prey fish
 streamer lures

individual fly names
Floating Fry *90*
floating lines *see* lines
fly boxes 13–14, *13,* 16
fly fishing
 blind 85, 87
 locales 16–17, 36–53
 see also
 loch fishing
 ocean fishing
 rivers
 stillwater
 streams
 origins 6
 tackle for 8–17, *18,* 93
 balanced 8
 care of 15–16
 tactics and techniques 72–95
 see also
 landing
 nymphing
 playing
fly lines *see* lines
fly tying silk 18–20
footwear 15, *15*
forceps 14, *14*
forward-taper (weight-forward) lines 10–11, 12, 24
Fraser, Gordon 48, 91
Fraser Nymph 121
front casting 24
Frying Pan River *28, 62, 80, 107*
Fujis *10*

G

Garry Dog *70,* 123
gastropods 57–59
 see also individual gastropod names
gillaroo trout 49
Glass Minnow 124
Glitter Spider 121
Gold Ribbed Hare's Ear 89, 119
Goofus Bug 70
Grafham 48
grayling *6,* 31, *32, 36,* 82
 arctic 31
grease 14, *14*
Greenwell's Glory 74
Greenwell's Glory Dry 113
Grey Duster 113
Grey Goose 119
Grey Goose Nymph *60*
Grey Nymph 119
Grey Wulff Mayfly 114
guides (rod rings) 10, *10,* 15, 22
 Fujis *10*
 keeper 22
 snake 10, *10*

H

Hairwing Blue Charm 123
Hairy Mary 123
Half Back 89
half-hitch 20
Harray, Loch 49
harry-longlegs *see* craneflies
hats 15, 25
Hawthorn 114
Helmsdale, River *43*
hollow backing 18
hooks 13, 94–95
humpback (pink) salmon 31
Humpy *69*

I

Imaginary Muddler 100–103, *102–103*
imagos 60
insects 59–69
 see also
 flies
 individual insect names
Invicta 115
Irresistable *69,* 110
Itchen, River *43*

K

keeper rings 22
Kennet, River *94, 101*
Killer Bug 56
king salmon *see* Pacific salmon
knots 18–22
 blood 22, *22*
 Cove (water) 21–22, *22*
 emergency nail *21*
 half-hitch 20
 loop-to-loop *21*
 nail 20
 needle 20, *20, 21*
 Palomar hitch *21, 22*
 sewn and whipped loop *21*
 tucked blood *22*
 whipped loop *21, 21*

L

lake fishing *see* loch fishing
Lambourn, River *6,* 72
landing 94–95, *94*
largemouth bass 32, *35*
leach patterns 75, *75*
leaders 12–13, *13,* 16–17
 attachment of 20–21, *20, 21*
 braid 20
 sinking 20
 tapered nylon 20
 twisted 20
Leven, Loch 49
Light Cahill 117
lines 10–13, *11,* 16–17
 care of 15
 double-taper 10–11
 floating 11–12, *11,* 20
 backing 12
 float-tip 12
 forward-taper (weight forward) 10–11, 12, 24
 grading 8
 materials 10–11
 running 12
 shooting-heads *see* shooting-heads
 sinking 11–12, *11*
 backing 12
 sink-tip 13
 weight 12
 winding on 20
 see also
 backing
loch casting *see* over-the-front casting
loch (lake, lough) fishing 48–49
 tackle for 17
loop-to-loop knot *21*
lough fishing *see* loch fishing
lures *see* streamer lures
Lyon, River *18, 36, 103*

M

MacMurray Ant 112
Mallard and Claret 74, 108, 115

FLY FISHING

March Brown 111
marrow spoons 14, *14*, 89
Mask, Lough 49
Mayflies (dayflies, olives) 59–61, *59, 60, 67, 69*, 88, 89
Melvin, Lough 26, 49, *50*
Michigan, Lake *31, 35*
Mickey Finn 122
midges (buzzers) 65–7, *65*, 88, 89, 91
'GT' 89
Missionary 56
Montana Nymph 117
Mosquito 111
mosquitoes 65
Muddler Minnow 56, 74, 122
muddlers 75, 90, 91, 100–103, *102–103*
muskellunge 31

N

nail knot 20, *21*
needle knot 20, *20*, 21
nets *14*, 15
Never-Never Nymph 103–104, *105*
northern pike 31, *32*
nymphing 59–60, 72, *84*, 87–89, *88*
river 83–86
stillwater 12, 86–7
nymphs 14, *63*, 70, 103–104, *105*, 117–121
hatching 85–86

O

ocean (sea) fishing 8, 12, 35
tackle for 17
olives *see* mayflies
Olive Scud 119
overhead casting 22–23, 24, *24*, 25
over-the-front casting 76
overtrousers 15

P

Pacific (king, spring) salmon (chinook) 29, 31, *31*, 91
Palomar hitch *21*, 22
Pale Olive Spinner 112
Peacock Spider 89
perch 32
yellow 32, *32*
Peter Ross 72–74
Pheasant Tail Dry 113
Pheasant Tail Nymph *60*, 120
pike
northern 31, *32*
pink salmon *see* humpback salmon
playing 93, *93*
Popping Bugs 71
pot-shooting 85
prawn 57
prey fish 54–57, *56*, 74, 90
priests 14, *14*, 95
Prince 118

R

rainbow trout 26, *26, 28*, 36, 48
Rat Faced MacDougall 70
records, keeping 16
Red Palmer 116
Red Spot Shrimp *56*
reels 12, *12*, 18
capacity 20
care of 15–16

multiplying 12
single-action 12
see also
braking
reel seats 10, 15
reservoirs *see* stillwater
retrieves 76–77, *78*–80, 88–89
Richard Walker Cranefly 114
rings *see* guides
Ringstead Grange *48*
rises 82, 83
rivers 39–45, *40, 41, 46*
tackle for 16, 17
tactics and techniques for 72–74, *74*, 81–82, 83–86
rod holders *15*
rod rings *see* guides
rods 8–10, 16–17
grading 8
handle 10
length 10
materials 8–10, *8*
roll casting *18*, 22, *23*, 25, *103*
Roman Moser's Arrow Points 95
Royal Wulff *69*, 110
Rutland Water 47, *47*, 48, 49

S

salmon 29–31, 36, *46*, 49, 91–92
Atlantic *28*, 29, *36*, 70, 91
dog (chum) 31
humpback (pink) 31
Pacific (chinook, spring, king) 29, 31, *31*, 91
silver (coho) 31, *31*
sockeye (blueback) 31
Salmon River *40*
Sawyer, Frank *56*
Sawyer, Swedish *60*
scuds *56, 57*
sea fishing *see* ocean fishing
sea trout 26, 36, 49
sedge flies *see* caddis flies
sewn and whipped loop *21*
Shipman's Buzzer (Midge) 120
shooting-heads 11, 12, 24, 45
backing 12, 20
shortlining 77
shrimp *56, 57*
shuck 67
side-casting 11, 24, *25, 76*, 77–78
silver (coho) salmon 31, *31*
single-haul casting 23–24
sinking agents 14, *14*
sinking lines *see* lines
smallmouth bass 32, *35*
snails 57–59
snake bite syringes 89
snake guides 10, *10*
Soca, River *93*
sockeye salmon 31, *31*
Soldier Palmer *70*, 116
sonneghan trout 49
sowbugs 57
Spey, River *44, 45, 74*
spinners 60
steelhead trout 26, *28*, 36, *40*, 68
steeple casting 25
stillwater 45–50, *46, 47, 48*, 90
nymphing 12
reservoirs 47–48, *48*
tackle for 17
tactics and techniques for 75–76, 82–83
see also

loch fishing
stoneflies 68, 69, *69*
Stonefly Nymph *68*
streamer lures 22, 71, 72–74, 75, *75*, 90, 122–123
streams 36–39, *39, 40, 45*
tackle for 16
sunglasses 14, *14*, 15, 25
Suspender Buzzer *65*

T

tackle *see* fly fishing
tarpon 35
Teal Blue and Silver 74, 116
Ted's Stonefly 118
Tellico 118
Test, River *43*
tippets 12–13, 16–17
top droppers 77, *77*
trailing 78
trout 26–29, *40, 41, 46*
brook (charr) *28, 29*, 36, 49
brown 26, *28*, 36, 49, 88
cut-throat 26, *28*
Dolly Varden 29
ferox 49
gillaroo 49
rainbow 26, *26, 28*, 36, 48
sea 26, 36, 49
sonneghan 49
steelhead 26, *28*, 36, *40*
tucked blood knot *22*
Tweed, River 45, *91*

U

underwear 15

V

vests 14–15, *14*
Vosso, River *28*

W

Waddington mounts 71, 91
waders 16, 45
wading staffs 15, *15*
waistcoats 14–15, *14*
Walker, Richard 60
water knot *see* Cove knot
Watten, Loch 49
weight-forward lines *see* forward-taper lines
whip finish 98–100, *101*
whipped loop 21, *21*
whippings 15
White Deceiver 124
Wickham's Fancy Dry 113
wind-trolling 78
Wonderland Wet Fly 104–107, *106*
Woolly Bugger 123
Woolly Worm 70, 89

Y

yabby *see* crayfish
Yellow Humpy 110
yellow perch 32, *32*
Yellowstone River *44*

Z

Zug Bug 118
Zulu 115